# THREE MILLENNIA

# AND

# COUNTING

## Women's Journey

## From

## Property To Equality

**Marilyn Duncan**

**Dedicated**

To my daughter

## Acknowledgements

I must first acknowledge my editor, Elizabeth Drake-Boyt. It would have been a different book without her expertise and guidance.

Next, I want to acknowledge my readers, Linda Duncan Davis and Charlot Martin, who helped shape the book with their insight; and Rev. Dr. Claudia A. Ramisch for technical assistance and persistent gentle prodding.

After that it gets harder, because all of the courageous women (and a few men) with whom I've worked, either as colleagues or survivors of abuse, have contributed to the writing of this book. I hesitate to use your names because of my fear of leaving someone out, but you know who you are. I am forever indebted to you for the support and comradeship you offered while we mutually engaged in difficult work. Whether we are staff, volunteer, or board member, it is the tight community of caring which makes it possible to continue.

And, of course, I would be remiss not to acknowledge my husband, DuWayne Keenan, for his enduring patience as I lose myself to the keyboard and play among the words. Love, always. . .

## Introduction

Although this book contains historical facts, it is not a book of women's history but focuses on the ongoing oppression of women and the violence which supports the oppression. These are my reflections and conclusions as I look back on the work I've done in the battered women's movement. I resisted writing them down for a long time as I resisted revisiting the pain in the stories.

But, even as I spent years of my life engaged with the community of people who work to end violence against women, I have not been able to ignore the wider problem. The oppressive tactics which keep women subordinate are not used on women alone. So this book is not for women only, but for anyone who has ever felt disenfranchised by an unyielding power structure.

Imagine a world; at peace, equally guided by men and women with no one concerned about the balance of power because all are confident they have enough.

# One

*"Men are afraid that women will laugh at them. Women are afraid that men will kill them."* -Margaret Atwood

My name is Ben. Five years ago I ran a warm bath for my wife, poured in bath salts and lit a candle in the bathroom. We had been fighting. She had bruises on her body from my fists and I wanted to make her comfortable.

After she climbed into the tub I pushed her head under water and held it there until she stopped breathing.

We had two children, twins, a boy and a girl. They were four. They were asleep in their beds. I smothered them one at a time with their pillows. I didn't want them to be sad about their mother or grow up without her. I intended to kill myself as well. I got a beer from the fridge to settle myself down. I decided to go for a drive then come back and shoot myself. But the minute I turned the ignition I knew I wasn't going back. I was arrested six days later, four hundred miles from home.

I am now serving a sentence of Life, without possibility of parole. I used to cry in the dark at night because I didn't have the guts to kill myself. But crying in prison is dangerous. There are worse things in life than dying; you can find most of them in prison.

My wife's name was Mary. We had been married six years when I killed her and at first everything was wonderful. I was head-over-heels in love with her and I thought she was with me too. But as time went on she started wanting to spend more time with her friends. And then she got pregnant. I loved my kids but I didn't like what they did to Mary. First they ruined her beautiful body and then it was "the kids need this, the kids need that, we can't go there because the kids need to go somewhere else," and on, and on. . .I guess this makes me sound like one selfish guy but, you see, I had never had anything of my own—anyone of my own—until Mary, and I felt like the kids were taking her away from me.

When I was growing up my dad took out all his frustration on my mom and me and my dad was a frustrated man. I had a younger brother but Dad never touched him, just Mom and me. I'd hear his car in the driveway and I'd cower in the farthest corner of the house, but if he'd had a bad day I could hear him taking his belt off even before he got to me. Mom was way too scared of him to try to help me. I'd sometimes think she was glad he was hitting me because then he wasn't hitting her.

I swore when I grew up I would never hit a woman or a kid. And I didn't until I felt Mary slipping away. Oh, I didn't think she'd leave me—at least not at first—but after a time I just didn't seem to be as important to her as I was in the beginning. It scared me a lot. And I guess I started knocking her around a little because I didn't know what else to do. Then, after the kids came along she just didn't care about my needs anymore and I panicked. I would have done just about anything to get things back the way they were in the beginning.

When the kids were about three years old I started getting a little rough with them too. Just a little, nothing like what my dad did to me. It was after one of those times, though, that Mary said she was looking for a job and after she found one she was taking the kids and leaving. That really set me off. I felt such rage I just couldn't stop hitting her. She couldn't leave the house again until those bruises healed and I could relax during that time. I didn't want to hurt her—I just wanted to feel in control—to not have to worry whether or not I was the most important thing in her life.

She told me she'd found a job the day I killed her. I couldn't stand to think of her anywhere but with me. I couldn't have faced the world knowing that she was in it but wasn't mine. I really planned to kill us all.

I've learned a lot in jail about domestic violence. There are other men in here who killed their women and a social worker comes and talks to us about what we did and tries to help us see why we did it. Some of the men may get out of here someday, but I'm not going anywhere. I'm sure I could find a way to kill myself in here, or get someone to do it for me, but I guess I still don't have the guts.

Am I sorry I murdered Mary? Sure, I wish I hadn't of had to do that but I still don't see any other way for me. I just could not have stood for her to have left me. When the social worker asks me to think of alternatives to what I did I can only think of two. I could have taken a gun and killed a whole bunch of other people but not Mary. I'm not sure how much that would have helped me. What I really think would have happened if she'd left me is that I would have curled up into a sniveling ball and never gotten up again—like waiting for Dad and that first crack of the belt—forever.

~

*My name is Mary. I fell in love with Ben because he seemed like the perfect guy. He was always attentive and loving and nothing I asked of him was ever too much. We got married six months after we met.*

*Things were still good for a while but after a few months I wanted to get together with my friends once in a while—*

*maybe once a month—and Ben didn't like that. He complained that I was putting my friends ahead of him. Actually, he complained no matter what I wanted to do without him. When I wanted to see my family I always asked him to come along and he never wanted to, but then he'd complain because I went without him. It was like he expected me to spend every minute with him and only him. It didn't happen often but several times he hit me after I'd been visiting with my family.*

*I thought it would get better after I got pregnant and he did stop hitting me but the complaints only got worse. I was sick a lot for the first few months and Ben seemed to resent it. I kept talking about the baby—I didn't know yet that we were having twins—and trying to get him excited about it, and he would say that he was, but at the same time he was irritated because I was sick all the time. Then after the babies started getting bigger, Ben complained about me losing my figure.*

*It wasn't very long after the twins were born before he started hitting me again. He complained that we didn't have a life together anymore. No matter how hard I tried to explain how much time it takes to care for two infants or how often I asked him for help, he never really got involved with the kids. It was as if there were the kids and me on one side and Ben on the other.*

*For a long time I didn't know what to do. He'd go for weeks without hitting me and then something would go wrong for him and I got smacked. At first he just slapped me; later on he used his fist. It was as though everything was my fault. Something could go wrong at work and he'd come home in a bad mood and hit me. I couldn't predict it and I also couldn't stop it.*

*I don't know how long I might have gone along with it; I really did love Ben, but he started smacking the kids around. I know Ben's history—how his dad abused him—and it really scared me when he started hitting our kids. He wasn't disciplining them, either, he was hitting them the way he hit me, for no particular reason other than he was having a bad day.*

*I was a nurse before Ben and I got married. I hadn't worked since we married because he didn't want me to. He said he always wanted to know where I was and to know that I'd be available to him. That had sounded sweet and loving when he first said it. Now I see it as something else.*

*After he started hitting the kids I told him I was looking for a job and as soon as I found one I was taking the kids and leaving him. He beat me so badly that I could scarcely move. For days I cried from pain while I took care of our children with no help from Ben, as usual. The kids asked what was wrong and I told them I'd fallen down the stairs but I'm pretty sure they knew the truth. It was a month before I was well enough to look for work, but my mind was made up the night he beat me. I would not stay with Ben.*

*It didn't take long to find a job. There is a shortage of nurses in my area and even though I haven't worked for six years I had two offers today and have accepted the one which will work best with the kids' schedule. I told Ben right after supper. He started hitting me but then he stopped. I'm bruised on my chest and stomach but not on my face, thank goodness, so I will be able to start work on Monday. I didn't mention leaving because I don't have a place to stay yet, but Ben has apologized for hitting me and is running a bath for me. I am hopeful that we can have a peaceful separation and get on with our lives apart. . .*

**YESTERDAY**
46 men in the United States murdered the women they had vowed to love.[1]

3,572 women were hit in their homes by an intimate partner.[2]

652 women were raped. 287 of them were under 18.[3]


**TODAY**
the numbers will be similar.


**TOMORROW**
they will be the same

and the day after that

and the day after that. . .unless. . .

# Two

*"Activism is the rent I pay to live on the planet."*
**-Alice Walker**

When the average woman goes out at night she attempts to park in a lighted area. If she is attending an event and expects there to be people coming and going, she may pick a parking garage. But she may also avoid one if she expects it to be mostly empty, because she recognizes that parking garages can be vast, anonymous, dangerous places for women alone.

She is warned to beware of parking next to vans in parking lots, especially if there is a man sitting in the van. And if she must walk a distance in the dark; be it on the street, in a parking garage, or a parking lot, she may very well be holding her car keys between her fingers because keys between fingers make a weapon to strike out at a potential attacker. Or she may have her finger on the panic button of her key, carry a loud whistle on her key chain, or hold pepper spray in her other hand. Some women will simply not venture out alone after dark.

By contrast, when a man goes out alone after dark he looks for the nearest parking space he can find regardless of lighting conditions. Unless the man moves about in a high crime area, or is a minority, he never gives a thought to his safety on the street day or night.

This difference is only one of the ways in which all women are held hostage by male violence. An individual woman may never be assaulted on the street or battered in her home but she knows the potential for violence against her exists and she modifies her behavior because of it.

It was my personal experience with the inequities that women face which first led me to work in the battered women's movement. But even my own experience had not prepared me for the terrible injustices suffered by many women. And—even more disturbing—the near total indifference to their suffering.

The movement was almost a decade old when I joined it. In the mid 1980's, I was doing outreach for a shelter-based program, organizing a response to domestic violence in several rural counties. I was hit with official denial—it isn't a problem for us—it doesn't happen here. The response was unified. Men from law enforcement, the justice system, and city administrations, (with a few notable exceptions) gave me a figurative pat on the head. But the patronizing was never more obvious than the day I sat in a rural district attorney's office.

I had called and made an appointment to speak with him. He knew I was there to talk about domestic violence. He stood to shake my hand but as soon as I was seated, he leaned back in his swivel chair, placed his feet, clad in cowboy boots, on his desk and drawled:

"Well, you know, it seems to me that women are just asking for it. I think they must like being hit."

Then he waited.

I was not the first woman who had come to his office to speak to him about his prosecution of domestic violence cases. The fact that showing the bottom of one's feet to a virtual stranger is a serious lack of respect in many cultures may or may not have been known to him at the time, but disrespect dripped from his honeyed tone and oozed from his laid out posture. He expected me to erupt with indignity at his remark.

Then I waited.

I never lost eye contact as the seconds rolled past. When I finally spoke, it was with as calm a voice as I could manage, and I told him that while I appreciated his sharing his point of view, I wholeheartedly did not agree with him. Slowly, he took his feet off his desk and sat upright.

Then we had a conversation.

I would like to say that from that day forward he was always pro-victim in his prosecution but I can't. He did, however, speak with me on several occasions regarding a victim or a perpetrator. It was a start.

When I sought out groups of women in the same rural communities, their response was much different from that of the officials. We would often meet in small groups in their homes, sometimes in their churches, libraries or offices. But they knew about the violence. It was happening to a friend; to a neighbor; to someone they loved; to them. When we first began talking they were surprised at the extent of the problem. They'd believed they were alone and that their abuse, or the abuses they only knew of from friends or family, were isolated incidents.

Slowly, the smaller groups began to meet together and ask for action from their officials. Today the battered women's movement has been professionalized, but in the early days it was ordinary women reaching out to other women, many of them having been battered themselves. They established volunteer crisis lines and, at times, sheltered women in their own homes in a true grassroots effort.

An example is a group of volunteer women in one of the counties where I was organizing. They had established a twenty-four hour hot-line for their community. In addition, they had developed a safe home system, meaning that they found people in the community who were willing to provide shelter in their homes for battered women and their children.

I was invited to attend one of their meetings and—as theirs was a sizable undertaking—I arrived expecting to find a sizable number of women there. Imagine my surprise when I found five women seated around a table. They assured me that except for one missing member they were it, the whole organization.

With the help of monks in a nearby monastery who were willing to call-forward a phone on a schedule provided by the women, these six women kept the line staffed. Their only expense was paying for the phone. This was in 1986.

They have since morphed into an organization called Crisis Connection, Inc., which covers six rural southwestern Indiana counties. I eventually worked there as a sexual offense services coordinator. Although it is now professionally staffed, Crisis Connection still relies heavily on the efforts of its volunteers, as do many other programs for domestic violence victims, because even now the need far exceeds the available funding.

Early in the movement, women's efforts were local and solitary because there was no unifying organization and no way to know what other women were doing in their communities. Not until the International Women's Year Conference was held in Houston in 1976 did women across the country really have access to each other and the opportunity to organize a battered women's movement nationwide.

In 1978 the National Coalition Against Domestic Violence was born. This organization emphasized gaining financial aid for shelters and grassroots services, sharing information, and supporting research. As a counterpoint, on May 23 of 1978, the U. S. House of Representatives failed to pass the Domestic Violence Act of 1978.

Even though more than seven hundred domestic violence shelters had been established in this country by 1983, there was still significant resistance—both at the public and private levels—to the idea of sheltering domestic violence victims or of prosecuting their batterers. Wife-beating was considered by many to be a family matter and services for victims were seen as meddling with the family. Law enforcement officers were trained in mediation for domestic violence calls, so their focus was on keeping batterer and victim together, at the risk to the victim of further violence after the officers left the scene. Mental health providers offered batterers the convenient excuse of uncontrollable anger, attributing the violence to individual pathologies rather than to issues of power and control.

Another component in the opposition to domestic violence service providers was the fact that lesbians in the feminist movement were often at the forefront of the battered women's movement; consequently there was a lot of "queer baiting" from such diverse sections of our society as religious groups and the Department of Justice. If you aren't familiar with the term "baiting" it's sort of guilt by association. If you are associating with Catholics, or Protestants, or comics, then *ipso facto* you must be a Catholic, or a Protestant, or a comic, or, in this instance, a lesbian. It's a tactic used to separate people who might otherwise be allies. And in this case it discouraged some straight women from getting involved who might otherwise have been supportive of the movement.

This is in no way a criticism of the lesbians' efforts. Their leadership was and is invaluable. It's simply an example of the inhospitable milieu in which everyone in the movement, gay and straight alike, worked in the 1980's.

Then, in June, 1994, a much loved national football hero, O.J. Simpson, was accused of brutally murdering his estranged wife, Nicole Brown Simpson, and her male companion, Ronald Goldman. During an eight month televised trial, Simpson's history of domestic violence was disclosed.

The jury acquitted him of murder. But the publicity had brought domestic violence forward into the public eye in a way that it might have taken years to otherwise accomplish. "Domestic violence" had become household words.

Also in 1994, the Violence Against Women Act was finally passed by the U.S. Congress and has been funded every year since then to provide grants to programs which shelter and advocate for women, prosecute perpetrators, and educate law enforcement and the public.

Today, more than forty years after the first shelter for women was established in this country:

- Protective laws have been passed.
- Shelter services for women and children have greatly expanded.
- Education programs have raised public awareness.
- Batterer's intervention programs (BIP) are available for court-ordered offenders.

Billions of dollars have been spent on the effort. Why, then, haven't the numbers of women being hit been dramatically reduced?

Could it be that our culture promotes the violence?

In not so subtle signals, our society reminds men of their duty to control women and women of their responsibility to acquiesce. The second wave of feminism may have taken us ". . . a long way, baby . . .," but we need only to critically observe our media content and advertising and to observe the inequity in the halls of power to understand that inequity is still being promoted and supported; sometimes by women as well as men. Some women have struggled to achieve equality but all women are still playing on the men's field, playing by the men's rules.

Attention is given to political correctness; but political correctness is form not function. A corporation executive may meticulously follow all the rules on how to treat women within his corporation while simultaneously hatching reasons not to elevate a competent woman past a certain level. The same executive may go home and act the tyrant, with or without physical violence, with his wife, daughters, and household staff.

What the average man on the street misses as he laughs at jokes about women and backslaps any manifestation of macho is that he is a tool in the grand plan. So long as half of the population can be held in conflict with the other half, energy and attention needed to correct the imbalances of class, race, and gender in our world will be diluted—to the detriment of his wellbeing as well as to that of women.

# Three

*"The past is our definition. We may strive with good reason, to escape it, or to escape what is bad in it, but we will escape it only by adding something better to it."* -Wendell Berry

So how did we come to this?

Many will say it is the natural order of things.

Many will say that man has always dominated woman.

Many will say that God ordained it and quote a holy text as proof.

They would all be wrong.

Historically, archeologists recognize a time when men and women lived in equality. Families were matrilineal: children were born into their mother's line and, if they were male, they remained in her household until she died and then joined the household of another female relative. If they were female, however, they stayed with their mother only until they had a child, which established their own line.

Some refer to this pattern as a matriarchal society but it isn't. A matriarchy or patriarchy refers to authority—who holds the power. There may have been some matriarchal societies in pre-history, as there have been a few in more recent times in isolated tribes, but there is no evidence that this was ever widespread, or that women ever dominated men as men have since dominated women.

Eventually men must have realized that they needed more children in order to have a strong tribe. For that they needed more women. Between 3100 BCE and 600 BCE an historic process took place. Women began to be stolen from their tribes, or, if the tribe had an abundance of women, they may have been bartered for food or other goods.

Did the women fight back? We simply don't know, but it would have been a futile fight, given men's superior body size and strength. Did the other women in their kin groups try to stop it? Or, did they help the men in their selection of who to trade, so long as it wasn't them, much as some women support men's violence today? They did not realize that in the process woman had become a commodity—an object sought for sexual privilege and her ability to bear children.

The anthropologist Claude Levi-Strauss identified the exchange of women as the leading cause of female subordination: "*The total relationship of exchange which constitutes marriage is not between a man and a woman. . . but between two groups of men, and the woman figures only as one of the objects in the exchange, not one of the partners.*"[4] From the moment of her birth, a woman was owned by and owed allegiance to a man—her father, if he lived, her brother or other male relative, if he did not. She owed this allegiance until her father or other male relative decided she should marry—and to whom—at which time her ownership was transferred to her husband.

The subordination of women, then, had been accomplished long before the major institutions on which our civilization is based were formed. Both the Bible and the Koran were written in a culture which had already accepted the premise that women are owned by men. All western thought has been based on this premise

We can look to the Bible to find proof of woman's total control  by her father: In Genesis 19: 7, 8, three strangers have come to Lot's house in Sodom. They prepare to spend the night but some of the Sodomites approach and demand that Lot send the strangers out to them that they might 'know' them. Lot's answer chillingly depicts his regard for his daughters:

*Behold now, I have two daughters that have not known man; let me, I pray you, bring them out unto you, and do ye to them as is good in your eyes; only to these men do nothing; forasmuch as they are come under the shadow of my roof.*

This verse has been used as a symbol of Lot's hospitality, but it also shows his complete ownership of his daughters. Lot has offered them, both virgins, to be raped by the Sodomites in order to protect the strangers (men) under his roof.

In a later millennium John Calvin, one of the founders of the Presbyterian Church, speaks:

*Certainly, it cannot be denied that the woman also, though in the second degree, was created in the image of God. We may therefore, conclude that the order of nature implies that the woman should be the helper of the man...The vulgar proverb, indeed, is, that she is a necessary evil; but the voice of God is rather to be heard, which declares that woman is given as a companion and an associate to the man, to assist him to live well.*[5]

So there's your choice according to Calvin: you may view a woman as a "necessary evil"—necessary for her reproductive and sexual services. Or, you may listen to the voice of God, which declares that woman is given as a companion to man "to assist him to live well"—whatever that should mean—as defined by the man, of course.

The belief in a man's ownership of his wife's sexual services was so strong that it wasn't until the 1970's that marital rape became illegal anywhere in the United States and it wasn't until 1993 that it became illegal in all states. Even today, some states' laws treat marital rape differently than they do acquaintance or stranger rape and the *Rape, Abuse and Incest National Network* (RAINN) reports marital rape as being infrequently prosecuted.

But just as women still suffer the effects of a three millennia old decision made by men, so do men today. The males in that earlier culture made a miscalculation. The enslavement of women by men was the precursor to the enslavement of men by other men. Instead of killing all the other men in battle as they had previously, the victors began to keep them as slaves, to do their bidding.[6] The men with the most slaves (wealth) became the leaders of their tribes and a class system based on power inequity was born. The things that divide us today, such as the inequity in gender, class, and race, may be seen as rooted in those early practices of enslavement: first, women; then, men; by those more powerful.

# Four

*"If we are to achieve a richer culture, rich in contrasting values, we must recognize the whole gamut of human potentialities, and so weave a less arbitrary social fabric, one in which each diverse gift will find a fitting place."* –**Margaret Mead**

Alice Paul first introduced an equal rights amendment to the U.S. Congress in 1923. President Dwight D. Eisenhower, the first president to support it, asked Congress to pass an equal rights amendment in 1958. The Republican Party had included the amendment in every one of their platforms since 1940 and the Democrats put it on their own platform after Congress passed it in 1972.

To become the law of the land it had only to be ratified by a majority of the states before the ten year deadline set by Congress. It was a simple amendment, sparse of language:

*Section 1.   Equality of rights under the law shall not be denied or abridged by the United States or by any State on account of sex.*

*Section 2.   The Congress shall have the power to enforce, by appropriate legislation, the provisions of this article.*

*Section 3.   This amendment shall take effect two years after ratification.*

That was the whole of it and ratification was progressing as state after state put it on their legislative agendas, so final passage was expected even though there was opposition from the AFL/CIO, at that time the strongest labor union in the country, and several other factions.

But the equal rights amendment failed to be ratified by the deadline because public sentiment changed. This simple amendment, meant to protect the rights of women, was mostly defeated through the efforts of one woman.

Phyllis Schlafly, an affluent conservative lawyer, is given most of the credit for spearheading the campaign that led to its defeat. She organized the STOP (Stop Taking Our Privileges) ERA effort and founded the conservative Eagle Forum. The amendment was demonized: rumors flew regarding its effects if it were to become law.

One rumor was that women would no longer be allowed to have separate restrooms in public places. There is no law now which gives women the right to separate restrooms; this is custom, not law. And have you ever ridden in a plane with separate restrooms? This allegation was simply made to frighten people—women—over the dreadful price they would pay for equality.

Another rumor was that our school systems would have to allow gay men and women as teachers in the schools and that these teachers would prey on our children and teach them to be gay—as if children could be taught homosexuality; as if homosexuals weren't already teaching in the schools and no likelier to be predators than the heterosexuals teaching there.

No matter how ridiculous, the hubris was successful in elevating women's fear; they climbed aboard Schlafley's bandwagon in sufficient numbers to defeat the amendment. How remarkable that an amendment which simply assures women's equality under the law should be defeated by women. Remarkable—but not really surprising.

Since the time of woman's historical fall from equality, she has had only one avenue to power—affiliation with and service to men. She could marry and hope that her husband would share what power he had with her—at the cost to her of her sexual and reproductive services as well as any material wealth she may have inherited. Or, she could serve the male gods in the temple and have some power in her own right, but, again, at the relinquishment of her sexual and reproductive freedom. She was often required either to remain a virgin or to provide sexual services to the priests.

Phyllis Schlafly, is herself an example of this kind of affiliation. Even in the 1970's when she was organizing STOP ERA, she had little in common with the women the Equal Rights Amendment could help the most. Married to an affluent man and with sufficient domestic help at home, she was able to pursue a career as a lawyer, raise six children, and travel the country making speeches. Her tradeoff of sexual and reproductive services was acknowledged by Schlafly herself in a March 2007 speech at Bates College when she answered a question about marital rape with: "By getting married, the woman has consented to sex, and I don't think you can call it rape."

Almost a millennium earlier, Lord Hale, an English jurist, had preceded Shlafly's sentiment when he said that when women married, they "gave themselves to their husbands" in contract and could not withdraw that consent until they divorced. The basis of the contractual consent theory is found in Hale's statement: "*The husband cannot be guilty of a rape committed by himself upon his lawful wife for by their mutual matrimonial consent a contract with wife hath given herself in this kind to her husband, which she cannot retract.*"[7]

This attraction toward affiliation still prevents women from trying, in sufficient numbers, the one thing that would almost guarantee them equality—solidarity. When women have tried to unite—as in the second wave of feminism in the 1960's-70's—the movement has been demonized in the same way as was the Equal Rights Amendment. One of the kinder things feminists were called was "ball busters," and women, dependent on men for their very livelihood, ran from the movement as fast as they could.

As one of those early feminists, and looking back with the clarity of hindsight, I can see that the movement itself was fragmented. There were strident voices, in tones of black and white with no shades in between, declaring: I woman—good, you man—bad. But there were also more reasoned voices seeking a different, kinder world, inclusive of both the sexes and benefiting men as well as women. Our mistake was in thinking we could do it by ourselves. Little attempt was made to bring the men along with us.

An incident from my personal life comes to mind and illustrates the point. I had traveled to Ireland with the man who is now my husband. In those days I was doggedly determined to take care of myself, by myself, and to that end I insisted on transporting my own luggage with no help from my male traveling companion.

The day of this incident had been particularly taxing and I was near the end of my strength. I may just insert here the information that my husband is 6'4" and I am 5'3" on a good day. On that day, he was becoming exasperated with my fierce insistence on my ability to do it all myself and he asked me why I so badly wanted to be a man. Upon which I burst out laughing: I enjoy being a woman, and would vehemently not want to be a man—it had never entered my mind. But was that what men thought we wanted?

In those days, as women struggled out from under dependence, we failed to recognize the value of healthy interdependence. In those days we failed to make ourselves clear to men—even to those who might have been able to understand. What I did want was to prove that I could be an independent woman; that I didn't need a man to live my life well, even though I might choose to share my life with one.

Women may point the way but we can't make a just world all alone. It will take all of us, men as well as women. But how can we hope to unite with likeminded men when the women themselves, are still sharply divided? The men were not the only ones we failed to include in the second wave of feminism. This mostly white, mostly middle-class movement also failed to include the specific and different concerns of women of color and women living in poverty.

It shouldn't be a competition. There are opportunities for all women; those who find their most fulfilling role in motherhood and home; those who strive to break through the glass ceiling, and all those whose desires, talents, and circumstances fall somewhere in between. We are not all— and should not strive to be all—alike. It's not even necessary that we all like each other. But we must include all women's concerns in our efforts.

# Five

*"I draw a line down the middle of a chalkboard, sketching a male symbol on one side and a female symbol on the other. Then I ask just the men: What steps do you take on a daily basis to prevent yourselves from being sexually assaulted?"* -Jackson Katz[8]

 A young female high school student was raped by two male members of her school's football team—sadly, a common occurrence. What brought this rape to national media attention was that it was successfully prosecuted and the young perpetrators went to jail—just as sadly, an *un*common occurrence. But it was what happened next that stirred up the most publicity and was debated on news channels for days.

Apparently, at least one of the perpetrators had a meltdown in the courtroom as he finally realized there were consequences for his actions—that he was going to serve time—his football career now ended as well as many of his options in life. And, apparently, his display of emotion overwhelmed one of the television reporters in the courtroom to the point of her reporting how very sad it was that these young men's lives and futures were now ruined. Not to be outdone, other television commentators jumped on that bandwagon and they all held a televised pity-party for the two rapists.

Hey—hold on—was there not a victim in the center of this? What about the impact on her young life?

What the reporters were exhibiting was a buy-in to rape culture. While the fact of rape culture is often denied, many key elements are apparent in this case:

### 1.Sympathy was given to the rapists.
Of course, they had ruined their young lives, but they had committed a violent act against the victim. Her scars didn't show but had they beaten her to the point of maiming her for life physically, rather than causing her lifelong mental anguish (ask any survivor of rape), would they have gotten the same sympathetic response?

### 2.What they did was viewed as a sexual act rather than a violent one.
Rape is an act of violence, born of male entitlement; carried out by male domination; applauded by many; and subtly accepted by many more. The argument is sometimes made— by men—that rape is just about sex. Rape is always an act of violence, albeit sometimes performed for sexual satisfaction by men steeped in the male mystique which tells them they shouldn't have to control themselves.

### 3.Protecting the rapist is the victim's responsibility.
After the verdict was handed down, two of the rapists' female friends were arrested for harassing the victim—they blamed her for getting the rapists in trouble by reporting the rape and testifying at the trial.

### 4. The victim is responsible for her own rape.
The thought of prosecution is so frightening to the victim that she may not consider cooperating in it. Everyone knows about victim blaming. And it doesn't stop with "getting the perpetrator in trouble"—it doesn't even start there. The victim is put under a microscope: Was she dressed provocatively? Had she gone alone to a questionable place? Was she drinking/drunk? Using/high? Flirting? It is assumed to be her responsibility to prevent her rape rather than the rapist's.

### 5. *It is also her responsibility to prove it.*

Rape victims are urged to undergo an exam through a rape kit; an invasive procedure which of necessity must be performed soon after the rape itself, because prosecutors won't prosecute on her identification of the rapist alone but demand DNA evidence as well as evidence that the rape actually took place. The word of the victim isn't good enough.

Even when a rapist is prosecuted and found guilty, justice is sometimes not served, as with the recent case of Austin Clem in Alabama who raped his victim when she was only fourteen and again when she was eighteen. He was convicted of one count of first degree and two counts of second degree rape. But when Judge James Woodroot sentenced him, he gave the rapist thirty five years, suspended, and put him on probation for five years. This example is so outrageous that it may eventually lead to the judge's ouster but it is only one of many lenient sentences against those who commit the crime of rape.

Rape is still being prosecuted against a history of treating rape as the theft of property. Indeed, the origins of the word come from the ancient Greek—to steal—and the theft was not seen as perpetrated against the woman but, rather, against her owner, such as her father or her husband.

It was not until the reign of Henry II in England, in the Twelfth Century, that women could file suit against their own rapists, and only if they were not married to them and only if they were virgins at the time of their rape. It was some two hundred years later, during the reign of Edward II, that English law acknowledged that a non-virgin could be forcibly raped so long as she was not married to the rapist. But, perhaps, even more importantly, at that time rape began to be seen as a crime against the state, in other words, a crime the state could prosecute rather than the victim having to personally bring forth a suit.[9]

In this country there is a clear connection between rape, racism and sexism. It was legal as well as common for white slave owners to rape enslaved women. A brave group of African American women who had been raped during the Memphis Riots, testified before the United States Congress in 1866. They were perhaps the first women in this country to speak openly about their sexual assaults.[10]

Racism was also apparent in the prosecution of rape, which was a capital crime only when a black man raped a white woman. White rapists faced lesser sentences for raping white women than black rapists and the rape of a black woman was not considered a crime, even when it became officially illegal.[11]

Society's denigration of women supports rape culture. Words like slut, bitch, whore—slurs that have no male equivalent—affect all women whether or not they are directed at us personally. Such slurs demean us all. The sexual harassment that occurs in our workplaces; the pay differential; the attitudes which either place us on a pedestal or relegate us to the gutter all serve to remind us that men are in charge and may do with us as they wish. This is rape culture. And because rape culture dictates that the shame of rape attaches to the victim, many women carry the scars of rape in secret to the very ends of their lives.

Men also suffer the trauma of rape and the stigma of being a victim. Men are even less likely to report it than are women, but the rape of males offers an example of how rape is an act of violence rather than an act of sex. Rape of males is often perpetrated by heterosexual males against other heterosexual males as an example that they are more powerful than their victims.

# Six

*"To control women, a man must sacrifice mutual love, trust, fellowship and intimacy and adopt an unremitting guarded stance of domination."* -**Marilyn French**

My name is Charlie. My fiancée, Emily, told me she was going out for dinner with friends but when she wasn't home by 8:00 and she didn't answer her phone I went to get her. Three hours is more than enough time for anyone to eat dinner.

I went to the restaurant where she said she was going but she wasn't there so I started tracking her, going to all the places she sometimes goes. I finally found her at the home of one of her friends. She was watching television like she had no place else to be. I was furious and asked her what the hell she thought she was doing. She started screaming at me. She said she had a right to go wherever she pleased and that I had no right to track her down.

I hit her once but she kept on ranting so I kept on hitting her. Shortly after that the police showed up. One of her friends called them. I tried to explain to the police that she had no right to go anywhere without letting me know where she was but they arrested me anyway.

~

I was working at the agency I spoke of in Chapter Two, Crisis Connection Inc., where I was offered the opportunity to train to become a Batterers' Intervention Program (BIP) facilitator. In 1998 I was certified in the Domestic Abuse Intervention Program (DAIP) of Duluth, Minnesota's model of BIP's, a model still in widespread use across the country. Crisis Connection put its own BIP into place, and I co-facilitated groups there for seven years. Charlie was in one of those groups.

BIP's seek to reeducate offenders. They attempt to undo the damage done by a misogynistic culture, one offender at a time. It's an uphill battle. A program has, usually, only two hours a week, for twenty-four to twenty-eight weeks, to counteract the results of years of growing up in a world which encourages and supports the entitlement of men in both subtle and blatant ways.

Let's hear more from Charlie as he moves through an assessment with me to determine his appropriateness for a batterers' intervention program:

~

I know I shouldn't have hit Emily but she still says I shouldn't have come looking for her and I'd like to know what I should have done instead. Am I just supposed to sit there waiting, not knowing where she is until she gets damn good and ready to come home?

I don't know what all the fuss is about, anyway. With her, with the police, with the judge. I'm not a batterer, I just knocked my fiancée around a little, and if she had kept in closer touch I wouldn't have had to do that.

I'm a nice guy, ask my neighbors, I help them out all the time. I've got a good job and I get along with everyone. I just don't understand why I need to be here talking to you much less coming to a group for 26 weeks. I'm not a criminal.

~

Charlie has in fact committed the crime of domestic violence battery despite his protestation of not being a criminal. His protestation of being a nice guy, however, is a perception about batterers that is often shared by the general public.

Just as they were in the 1990's when their hero, O. J. Simpson, was revealed as a batterer, people today are startled to learn that their neighbor, co-worker, or friend has been arrested for domestic battery. "But he is such a nice guy. I can't believe he'd do that."

The myth is that otherwise 'nice guys' don't hit women. Most of the men going through a BIP would fall somewhere along a continuum between mostly nice and very nice with their friends and neighbors. Rarely are they know as violent men.

Most batterers don't hit their neighbors, coworkers, friends, or annoying strangers when they're angry at them, which dispels the myth of uncontrollable anger sometimes used as an excuse for domestic violence. Often their anger is so controlled that they only hit their wives or girlfriends in areas of the body covered by clothing, thus allowing her to go to work and about her daily life with no one suspecting she's been beaten.

A man, who may be known as a nice guy in every other area of his life, may still be abusive to a wife or girlfriend because of his deeply held beliefs. He must believe he has a right she does not have—the right to be in control. If he believes part of what it means to be a man includes controlling her, any show of independence on her part may threaten his self-perception as well as trigger fears that she will leave. He will go to any lengths necessary to keep her there—sometimes unto death as we saw with Ben in the first chapter:

"I couldn't stand to think of her anywhere but with me. I couldn't have faced the world knowing that she was in it but wasn't mine."

Until there is general acceptance that even nice guys do hit women, abusers will continue to hide behind their facade of niceness. What's needed is publicity, not only about the problem of domestic violence—although some people are still in denial about that—but of the offenders themselves.

During the 1980's, Mothers Against Drunk Driving (MADD) initiated a campaign to publicize the arrest of drunken drivers. Many newspapers cooperated and published the names of drivers arrested, some on the front page of their papers. The threat of being publicly ostracized changed the drinking and driving habits of many. If batterers knew we would find their names prominently placed on our media of choice, would they think twice before committing violence? And they could think twice. Between stimulus and response there is always a moment of choice.

Along with the ostracism, offenders need to be assured of swift and just legal action. From the arresting officer to the judge on the bench, all must be convinced that a crime has taken place. This is sometimes not the case.

Until the violence ends, everyone loses. The victims lose safety, homes, stability for themselves and their children—but the abusers lose as well. Charlie lost the good regard of some of the coworkers and neighbors who once knew him only as a nice guy, although, sadly, others among those coworkers and neighbors are probably applauding his actions, claiming that a man has got to keep a woman in line, no matter the consequences. But most importantly for Charlie, he lost the love and respect of the woman he loved and wanted to marry.

~

*My name is Emily. I was in love with Charlie, maybe I still am, but I've broken our engagement and moved out of the house. My family is upset about this. They think Charlie hung the moon and they think I should overlook his behavior. He hit* me but my mother thinks I should overlook it because she thinks Charlie is such a nice guy and such a good catch.

She thinks I should give Charlie a second chance but what she doesn't know is that this was Charlie's second chance. He'd hit me once before. I guess I should have left then but I loved him and believed him when he said it would never happen again.

It wasn't only that he hit me though. He was getting more possessive as time went on. He had accused me of wanting to have an affair with one of my coworkers. And the night he was taken to jail I had clearly told him that my girlfriends and I would probably do something after dinner and not to expect me home until about ten o'clock. I wouldn't just not show up because I know how he is and I would have told him everything we'd done when I got home. I wasn't hiding anything.

I won't go back, no matter what my family says. I won't live like that and I no longer believe Charlie when he says it won't happen again. I hope I never see him again.

# Seven

*"Historically, groups of people have established and sustained supremacy over other groups of people by the use of violence that includes ongoing and systemic patterns of intimidation, coercion, as well as other tactics of control to physically, morally, spiritually, and economically devastate them." -Ellen Pence, Shamita Das Dasgupta[12]*

Domestic violence is illegal in every state in the country but only the physical acts of violence are prosecutable. Women who stay with physically abusive partners know in their deepest selves that the abuse is wrong even though they may make excuses for the abuser. Women who stay with emotionally abusive partners, however, may end up doubting their own sanity.

~

My name is Frank. I only waved a gun at my ole lady and now the judge says I have to go to these classes for twenty six weeks. He says I have to pay for them. That's not fair. If he's making me go he should pay for them himself.

First thing I get into the class they tell me I got to stop calling my ole lady my ole lady. Like all of a sudden she's too good or something. I didn't do anything to her. I told her she was a lazy fat slob and to clean herself up. Geez! She had baby spit-up all down the front of her shirt. And the house smelled like dirty diapers from the other two kids. The oldest is two and a half and should be out of diapers anyway.

My ole lady has it good. She only works part time since the three month old was born and the least she can do is keep the house and kids clean enough that I don't have to smell them. She yelled at me and told me to clean up the diapers myself and I pulled a shotgun and threatened her with it. I never touched her.

~

A useful tool in BIPs is the *Wheel of Power and Control.* The *Wheel's* rim is *Physical and Sexual Violence.* Its hub is *Power and Control.* The spokes form eight pie shapes with the headings of:

- *Using Intimidation*

- *Using Emotional Abuse*

- *Using Threats and Coercion*

- *Isolation*

- *Minimizing, Denying & Blaming*

- *Using Children*

- *Using Male Privilege*

- *Using Economic Abuse*

The Domestic Abuse Intervention Program (DAIP) from Duluth, Minnesota, developed the wheel after battered women reported emotionally abusive and controlling behaviors that were ongoing between episodes of actual physical violence. So it was the battered women, themselves, who supplied the lists of behaviors in the pie shapes.

Most men are confounded when they first see the behaviors listed by the women because they never considered them to be abusive; this is just the way normal men behave; the way their fathers behave; the way their friends behave. From that point on, the job of a BIP facilitator is to ask them to identify their abusive behaviors of choice, to consider why those behaviors are abusive and how they might change them.

Frank exhibits several of these behaviors: most specifically, *using emotional abuse* in his name calling, like "lazy fat slob" and "ole lady" and *using threats and coercion* by threatening her with a gun. He also admits to using *intimidation:*

~

I would never hit a woman. I've smashed things to get her attention and I put my fist through the drywall once or twice. I also took a shovel and smashed the windshield once when she took the car out and didn't come home when she was supposed to. But I've never hit her.

This time I just waved the gun around because it took a lot of work to fix the drywall and money to fix the windshield and I didn't want to go through that again. I didn't think waving the gun would cost me anything, but now I have to pay for these classes. I didn't even think the gun was loaded, although when the cops came they said it was.

~

*Intimidation,* then, exerts control by acting in ways to elicit fear. When a man smashes the wall the message is that he could just as easily smash his victim but it is indirect.

*Threats and coercion,* by contrast, promise direct action. "I have this gun in my hand and I will use it on you if you don't do as I say." The threat here is evident but her belief in the threat is the coercive factor.

Threats may take many forms. As in the example above, threats of physical violence may carry a lot of weight with a victim who has already been hit. Threats to take the children from her or threats to commit suicide may be empty threats, but they are believed by the victim because when she remains with an abuser for a time, she loses all perspective. Her constant fear of abuse and her experience, common among victims, of "walking on eggshells" to try to prevent further abuse and being abused anyway, make her feel helpless. At the same time she believes that her abuser is all powerful, almost omnipotent.

A batterer may also threaten: "If I can't have you, no one can." Unfortunately, this is not always an empty threat. The most dangerous time in a battered woman's life with an abuser is when she leaves him. As it was with Ben in the first chapter, her determination to leave, or her actual departure is the ultimate loss of control for him. This is also the point at which batterers may make good on the threat of suicide which Ben in the first chapter said was his intention:

"I intended to kill myself as well. I got a beer from the fridge to settle myself down. I decided to go for a drive then come back and shoot myself. But the minute I turned the ignition I knew I wasn't going back. I was arrested six days later, four hundred miles from home."

*Emotional abuse*, on the other hand, such as the name calling Frank uses: "lazy fat slob", and "ole lady" instead of using her name, is the slow drip, drip which erodes a victim's self-confidence and makes it easier for him to control her.

Emotionally abused women often say that they almost wish they were being hit. When they are hit, they know it. On the other hand, when they are bombarded by hurtful words and psychologically damaging games, it can be difficult to define—even to themselves—what exactly is going on.

There is an insidious assault against their sense of self and their self-esteem. Constantly repeated terms like "dummy" or "hippo" as terms of pseudo-endearment, change their perception of themselves. Statements such as: "you know you're no good at math"; or, "you know you're no good with directions—you couldn't find your way to the corner store"—change their perception of their abilities.

Of course, not all emotional abuse is that blatant; some instances can be very subtle and may even be mistakenly attributed to the abuser's personality.

### The Improver
Regardless of the intelligence and competence of his victim, whatever plan the victim suggests, the Improver will tell her how to improve it—or herself—or her appearance—or her outfit. Just a little, mind you, just for her benefit.

### The Strong Silent Type
Disagrees with pretty much everything his victim says and does, but he'd never tell her directly what, specifically, he doesn't like. He will, however, close up like a clam and sit around with a pained look on his face no matter how much the victim pleads with him to tell her what's wrong—or, worse—insist that everything is fine even though his actions and demeanor say otherwise.

### The Smiling Man, aka, The Passive Aggressive Man
Also insists everything is fine but at the last minute has misplaced the tickets to something his victim has been looking forward to. Or he forgets the important date, or that he had promised to come home early to look after the kids so she can keep an appointment or spend time with her friends.

Every abuser will have his own variation of tactics—or a different pattern altogether. In truth, most of us can pick out a few of our favorite tactics from the *Wheel* which we may use on occasion to temporarily get our way. But an abuser will use them as Frank did, in a consistent ongoing pattern with the intention to permanently control his victim's behavior.

~

*My name is Sally. I'm also known as Frank's "ole lady". His whole family calls me that. Actually, that may be one of the nicer things Frank calls me.*

*It seems I can do nothing right. I have three kids and work part time. Frank expects everything at home to be picture perfect and he does nothing. Nothing but scream at me about whatever his new favorite complaint is and call me names.*

*I work in a supermarket as a checker so I'm on my feet all day; even if it is just for a five hour shift I'm tired when I pick up the kids and then have to hurry home to try to get the house clean enough that Frank isn't going to complain. And the kids clean enough and quiet enough. And the laundry done. And try to guess what food he's going to want to eat that night and have it hot and ready when he gets home.*

*I can never seem to get it all right enough for him. I cry at night after Frank's asleep and I'm always scared. Scared that I haven't done it right, whatever it is. Scared that one of these days Frank will hit me. Sometimes I wish he would, maybe then I could show people and they would understand how miserable my life is.*

*I've talked to my boss at the market about working fulltime as I did before my last baby was born but it still won't be enough money for me to take the kids and leave. I'll have to work a second job and I don't know if I can do it and still take care of my kids right. I feel trapped and don't know what to do.*

# Eight

*"Love is when I am concerned with your relationship with your own life, rather than with your relationship to mine. . . .There must be a commitment to each other's well-being. Most people who say they have a commitment don't: they have an attachment. Commitment means, 'I am going to stick with you and support your experience of well-being.' Attachment means 'I am stuck without you.'* -Stewart Emery

Next to *Emotional Abuse* on the *Power and Control Wheel* is *Isolation.* A strong support system is the best defense against abuse, and *isolation* of his victim may be an abuser's first tactic. Especially for emotionally abused victims, having a strong support group of friends and family can serve as a reality check. No, she isn't going crazy. There really is something wrong going on here.

~

My name is Ed. I am not a violent man, Carol and I have seldom even had a cross word and I certainly would never lay a hand on her. But this one night we were fighting and I just got so mad I picked up a cut glass punch bowl, a hideous thing that Carol's aunt left her, and I smashed it hard against the sink and kept smashing it until it finally broke. By this time Carol was screaming and the neighbors had called the police.

I still think I could have explained everything to the police except that when the glass broke a couple of shards flew up and cut Carol's cheek. I tried to explain to the police that I hadn't meant to hurt her but she had to have stitches and I got sent to jail. The judge couldn't seem to understand, either, when I explained that her getting cut was just an accident, so now I have to go to these groups for six months.

~

*Isolation* often begins with criticism of the victim's supporters which may be as insidious as the emotional abuse of the victim. The slow drip, drip of her friends' or family's supposed shortcomings every time she suggests spending time with them, may disincline her to see them at all. If criticism doesn't do it, jealousy may.

~

So the funny thing is, in this group they're talking to me about all this stuff that men shouldn't do. And one of the things we shouldn't do is to isolate our wives—and I know exactly what they're saying. I used to have to know what Carol was doing every minute of the day. I just love her so much that I couldn't stand not to know all her thoughts and feelings, and where she was. And she was fine with it. Oh, maybe at first she grumbled a little about having to give up some of her ditzy women friends, and shopping with her mom who always convinced her to spend too much.

~

An abuser's protestations of such great love that he can't stand for her to be away from him can be flattering—at first. Jealousy is often mistaken as a sign of love, but jealousy is not about love. Jealousy may be used as a tool for control by the abuser, but it is always more about the insecurity of the jealous one than it is about love for the other.

There is an element of *isolation* in most offenders' stories. An abuser may become so efficient at isolating his victim that she spends every waking moment, outside of working hours, with him, doing only the activities he enjoys. He may even monitor what she reads and the television she sees and eventually control what she thinks by suggesting what is right and appropriate. Indeed, some victims become so dependent on the abuser they become complicit in their isolation and complain on the occasions the abuser may make other plans for himself.

~

That's not the funny part though, the funny part is that I had a job change about a year ago and I met these cool guys at work. They're married like me but they get together at the sports bar to watch the games and just hang out. I want to spend some time with them but Carol is throwing a fit about it. She's gotten all clingy and demanding and wants me to spend all my time with her like I always have. That's what the fight was about.

The people in this batterer's intervention program say that Carol has as much right to see people and do things without me as I have a right to see people and do things without her. I still love Carol, I just want a little breathing room. But I guess Carol has forgotten how to breathe without me--and I guess that's my fault.

~

*My name is Carol. I used to be an interesting woman, at least that's what my friends said. Sadly, I don't have any friends left. Ed and I have been married for seven years and for at least the last five I have spent my every waking moment except for work, with Ed.*

*We were so much in love and Ed wanted me to spend all my time with him. At first I kept seeing friends but every time I did he disparaged them. I couldn't see it at the time but every time I was going out with them he'd have some negative remark to make about one or the other. And sometimes I'd have plans with friends and Ed would come up with his own plans for me and expect me to cancel mine. And I would because I loved him and didn't want to upset him. Eventually I just gave up trying to go out without Ed. Eventually my friends stopped calling.*

*So now Ed has new friends and he goes out with them three or four times a week after work. And he's complaining because I'm complaining. He says we never fought and he's right. That's because whatever Ed wanted he got. Now he wants me to make new friends—it's not that easy.*

# Nine

*"You must begin by assuming responsibility. And you alone are responsible for every moment of your life, for every one of your acts." -***Antoine de Saint-Exupéry**

My name is Mike. I only touched my girlfriend, Denise, with two fingers and I don't know what the big deal is. Denise is the one who started the whole thing. She is the one who should be here, if anyone should.

I came home from work tired from too much overtime and I'd just walked through the door when she jumped my case about not moving some trash away from the garage door. Sure, I promised to move it, and she can't get her car out of the garage until I do, but she doesn't need to be out running around anyway.

We pretty much argued through dinner, about one thing or another, but after she took our two boys in to put them to bed I chilled in front of the TV. I was feeling pretty mellow until she came back into the room and started yelling all over again. I stood up and put my fist through the wall. That calmed her down but it really got my blood to boiling. I would have left the house but she was in my way and I had to move her over.

I guess the police have pictures of some bruises on Denise's neck and that's why I'm here.

~

This was Mike's story when he first came to the BIP. When I asked him how hard it is to cause bruising with a two fingered touch, he mumbled that it was all her fault, that he wouldn't have had to touch her at all if she'd just gotten out of his way.

Mike is using domestic violence perpetrators' favorite excuses: *Minimizing* the abuse. *Denying* that anything happened. *Blaming* the victim for causing the abuse.

*Minimizing*: I only touched her with two fingers.

*Denying:* By implication: how hard could a two fingered touch be?

*Blaming:* If she had only gotten out of my way I wouldn't have had to touch her.

*Minimizing, Denying, Blaming* fill another space on the *Power & Control Wheel.* Until the perpetrator takes responsibility for his actions there is no hope his behavior will change.

~

*My name is Denise. I am living with Mike, but only for a short time longer. I just rented my own apartment. I should have done it a long time ago. All Mike has ever done for me is give me two kids. It's been my responsibility to figure out how to keep our lives on track in every possible way.*

*He'd been promising to move the stuff from in front of the garage door for a week. I'd been borrowing rides from the neighbors and family to see that my kids and I got to where we needed to go. Our whole lives together have been like that.*

*Mike will procrastinate until the issue is no longer a problem because his family has found other rides, his co-workers have done the work—or straightened out the mess—for him, or people have just stopped expecting he'll do what he says he'll do. I'm tired of making up excuses and covering for him.*

*When he tried to choke me it was the final straw for me. He says he barely touched me; the bruises on my neck say otherwise.*

~

My name is John. I shouldn't be here, even Lisa agrees the argument was all her fault. She'd been out shopping with her sister which is always bad news. Her sister puts delusions of grandeur or something into her head and she always ends up buying stuff she doesn't need.

Usually she agrees to take the stuff back to the store but this time she kept arguing that she really wanted to keep a pair of sexy shoes, like she needs sexy shoes, and I finally pushed her and she fell. She got up and ran into the bedroom and I followed her and slapped her hard to get some reason back into her head. I guess she fell again, anyway after I left the room she called the cops.

Just as soon as the cops got there, she realized what a mistake she'd made in calling them but they took pictures of a bruised cheek and some carpet burns on her legs and that's what got me here. But, believe me, Lisa is very sorry about all of this. She knows what a mistake she made; she feels a lot of guilt over my having to come to this program.

~

It's an old story to the police: a woman calls to report abuse only to say that nothing really happened when the officer arrives. A victim may have made the call in real fear but now the fear of further abuse from the perpetrator, if she cooperates with the police, may be greater.

~

*My name is Lisa. As soon as I called the police I knew I had made a mistake. I can usually handle John's abuse but that night he really scared me. As soon as I'd made the call, though, I was even more scared—scared John would kill me. I tried to tell the police nothing really happened but all they needed to do to know that was a lie was look at me. I was covered with bruises.*

*Now he has to go to those classes and he holds it over me constantly. He almost always comes home from them and hits me. I'm supposed to tell someone if he hits me while he's in the program but he'd just get out of jail again and it would be worse than ever. I'm afraid to leave him. Wherever I'd go, he'd find me.*

~

As in rape culture, a victim of domestic violence is often blamed for the violence, by both the perpetrator, and by the larger society. A perpetrator is only too willing to give her the blame.

If only she had dinner waiting; or his laundry done; or could keep the kids quiet, he wouldn't have to hit here. Or, if only she hadn't spent too much money; spent too much time on the phone; or forgotten to buy his favorite food, he wouldn't have to hit her.

But society, too, often blames women if their relationships are violent. There must be something the woman could do to fix the relationship; it must be something she is doing wrong— which nicely echoes the abuser's message. And, as a woman grows up, she absorbs a society's expectations that the health of a relationship is her responsibility. She is often as ready to believe the abuse is her fault as the abuser is to reinforce her belief.

In BIP's, then, a facilitator's hardest task may be to convince an abuser that he is solely responsible for his abuse. That he must give up *minimizing, denying, and blaming.* It doesn't help the facilitators' efforts or the abuser's understanding when community officials, those we would like to believe adhere to a higher standard, use the same tactics.

In 1996, a judge in New York, Judge Lorin Duckman, asked the young woman before his bench, "There is no actual physical injury, is there, other than some bruising?" And he continued, "I'm not suggesting bruising is nice, but there is no disfigurement. There are no broken bones." The Judge's *minimizing* led him to release the perpetrator without bail. The perpetrator killed the young woman less than three weeks later.[13]

Although the above is an eighteen year old case, in late January, 2014, Senator Chuck Grassley of Iowa said: "I'm concerned that the absence of mandatory minimum sentencing is causing serious problems in deterring these terrible acts of sexual assault and domestic violence." Apparently, not a lot has changed in the past eighteen years. Although Grassley was successful in including mandatory minimums to a federal bill, most states' laws allow a lot of judicial discretion in sentencing domestic violence perpetrators.

As long as the crime of domestic violence is being denied: "it doesn't happen here;" minimized: "bruising really isn't that bad;" or blamed on others: "if she would change I wouldn't have to hit her;" abusers evade responsibility and the violence continues.

# Ten

**"Male privilege is not granted by nature, God, or chromosomal differences; it is something that men have built into the structure of society and that they fight to maintain. . ." -Ellen Pence & Michael Paymar**[14]

My name is Tony. I shoved my wife, Sheila, into a wall during an argument. She hit her head and shoulder and called the police. By the time they got there her shoulder was bruising and there was a knot on the back of her head. I guess that was what got me arrested.

We were arguing about money. That's all we ever argue about. Sheila likes to shop and would spend every cent we make on God knows what kind of junk that we don't really need, that she doesn't need. I know we'll never get ahead unless we save but she accuses me of being a Scrooge and just won't stop spending. Worse yet, she keeps quitting jobs, so most of the time it is my money she's spending.

~

The idea of partnership and shared resources is foreign to most men who come into BIP's, as can be seen in Tony's opinion that when Sheila spends money he has earned she's spending *his* money.

~

The fight started when I told her I was cutting her off the credit cards and check book. That from now on it was going to be my way or the highway. I told her that If she wanted something she could ask me for the money but unless it was for food she had little to no chance of getting it.

~

One of the most difficult segments of the *Power & Control Wheel* for abusive men and the general public, alike, to understand, is the one that deals with male entitlement. Because male privilege is so tightly woven into the fabric of society it is almost invisible, you may miss the signs altogether unless you remain constantly aware, but male privilege affects every woman's life. On the surface Tony's problems seem to be caused by money, but if we take a closer look we see that Tony believes in his right to deliver ultimatums to his wife.

~

After I came into this program they told me that as my life partner Sheila had a right to have some say over how the money is spent. Pissed me off big time. I skipped two meetings but I came back because these people report my attendance to the judge and I can go back to jail if I don't come to these meetings. Then they asked me a question I had to think about. They asked me if my behavior toward Sheila is getting me what I want.

What I want is a loving wife and family. What I want is peace. What I want is to save enough money to buy a house and get ahead but I can't do that while Sheila is spending all the money.

~

Only after Tony was challenged to think about whether his tactics were getting him the life he wanted was he able to consider that there might be another way to be in a relationship; a way which did not demand that he be in control. Male privilege just feels natural—to many women as well as to most men.

~

In another meeting we did some role playing on communication and I thought, well, what do I have to lose? I sat down with Sheila and explained to her what my goals are for all of us, why I object to her spending. And she told me how she felt growing up really poor, and how it makes her feel to be able to spend on things she likes.

We talked and talked and I was surprised at how quickly Sheila came around to my way of thinking when I really explained how I felt about saving money. We finally agreed to save some out of every paycheck, mine and hers, and agreed that there will be a little each month for her to spend as she likes. She is looking for a new job and she says she intends to keep it because she now wants to help save for a house of our own, something she's never had.

~

*My name is Sheila. Tony and I used to fight all the time, mostly over money. He was always on me to get a better paying job and to spend less. When he hit me I called the cops. Tony had to go to jail and then he had to go to a batterer's intervention program. It really pissed him off. He insisted he wasn't a batterer.*

*For a while things were worse. He never touched me again but he snarled about everything. Then, all of a sudden, one day he asked if we could talk. I thought, all he ever does is talk, but he really did mean talk to each other. And when I talked, he really listened. That had never happened before.*

*Now things are different. We still don't always see eye to eye and we still argue sometimes but most of the time we sit down and talk it out. Tony has never again hit me.*

My name is Joe. I am 47. Bethany is my 41 year old live-in girlfriend. We never had any trouble over money. Bethany makes more than I do; she's worked really hard and has a great job in management, but her making more doesn't bother me at all. I don't care who makes the money or who manages it.

Bethany was married once and has two grown-up kids. I've never been married. Our trouble started after Bethany got pregnant. I was ecstatic. I've always wanted a child and at 47 I didn't think I'd ever have the chance but there it was—in Bethany's belly. I couldn't have been happier and I planned to marry Bethany.

The week after she found out she was pregnant Bethany told me she was going on a trip with her girlfriend for a couple of days. She said they wanted to do some shopping and I thought they'd shop for stuff for the baby. Instead, when they got back Bethany wasn't pregnant anymore. She'd gotten an abortion. She told me she wasn't interested in starting another family at age 41 or in marrying me.

I lost it. How dare she get rid of my child. We screamed at each other for hours. I was in so much pain that I wanted Bethany to know what it felt like. I pulled out a hunting knife and threatened to cut her with it just as she had cut my baby out of herself.

I wouldn't have really done anything to her but she called the police. I just wanted her to know what I felt like. I just wished she'd told me what she intended to do because I would have prevented that from happening even if I had to keep her locked up until the baby was born.

~

*My name is Bethany. Joe is pulling this big act about being so wounded because I had an abortion. I told him from the very first time we talked about getting together that I had raised my family and had no intention of having another child. There could have been no doubt in his mind as to my position on this.*

*I was on birth control but started having some health problems and the doctor took me off of them. I warned Joe again that he needed to be really careful with the condoms because there was no way I was having another child. So now he's all dramatic about how I got rid of 'his' baby. I didn't like having an abortion. In fact, I feel bad about it, but I'm forty one and I don't want to spend the next twenty years of my life raising children.*

*I also feel bad about calling the police on Joe but I was seriously scared of him. He kept ranting that he should have locked me up until the baby was born. And then he threatened me with a knife.*

*The two of us are over. I've moved out. I hope Joe gets the help he needs but I could never trust him again and I'm sure he'd say the same thing about me.*

~

My name is Milford. I shouldn't be in this program. Neighbors called the cops because they heard me yelling at my wife, Jenny, who hasn't learned to cook a decent meal in the seven years we've been married. That's when she cooks it fresh, but the night the cops were called she'd put warmed up leftovers in front of me even though she knows I can't stand leftovers. I guess I went a little beyond the yelling because when the cops came they took a picture of a red mark on the side of Jenny's face and took me to jail.

You'd think she would have learned something from having caused me to go to jail. You'd think she'd try harder, but, no.

The house is still the same pigsty it's been for seven years. The food is just as bad. My shirts still aren't ironed the way I like them. Useless, Jenny is just useless. She does manage to hold on to a job so I suppose she must do something right, but the job's not much. She works full time and makes about half my salary. But she just won't listen to me when I tell her she has to change so what am I supposed to do?

The judge said I have to come to this program and the people here have the nerve to ask me why I don't do some of those things myself if I don't like the way Jenny does them. I don't know how to do any of those things. Why, in hell, should I? That's women's work.

~

*My name is Jenny. I guess I'm not the best housekeeper and cook in the world but I seriously doubt that anyone could please Milford. Believe me I've tried.*

*The night the police came was not the first time he's hit me it's just the first time anyone called the police. That was an eventful day in my life. I'd worked half a day because I knew if I didn't Milford would complain about the reduction in my pay. He'll complain anyway but it won't be as much as if I'd taken off all day.*

*At noon I went to the hospital to be with my mom who had surgery for breast cancer scheduled for one o'clock. I stayed at the hospital until she was out of surgery and I could talk to her in recovery but then I had to leave to get Milford's dinner. Traffic was heavy and I didn't get home in time to cook; we had nice leftovers from a pot roast the day before and I warmed those up thinking he would understand since my mom had just had surgery.*

*Everyone says I should leave him. We don't have kids to keep me here and honestly I don't know why I stay. Maybe I feel a little sorry for Milford; I don't know how he'd survive alone.*

A favorite phrase for many men in batterer's groups is, "Somebody has to be in charge," and the 'somebody' to whom they refer is themselves. They have never considered the concept of shared responsibility with an equal partner. Tony, Joe, and Milford have very different issues but they all exhibit a belief in *male privilege*. Tony was the only one of the three who eventually got it right. In my years working with the BIP, I never met an abuser who did not have a firm belief in *male privilege.*

# Eleven

*"All over the place, from the popular culture to the propaganda system, there is constant pressure to make people feel that they are helpless, that the only role they can have is to ratify decisions and to consume."* **–Noam Chomsky**

The behaviors listed between the spokes of the *Wheel of Power and Control* are found everywhere within our society. One need not ever be battered in a relationship to experience them; these same behaviors are typically used by the government and corporate power structures to maintain control of all of us.

For as long as law has existed, men have passed laws to protect their own sovereignty *(male privilege)*. When the preamble to our constitution was written, ". . .all men are created equal. . ." meant exactly what it said—all men; women could not vote, married women could not sell their inherited property without the permission of their husbands. To be even more precise, it meant all *white* men of property, for only they had a vote.

So long as men in positions of power make decisions which affect only women—without equal representation from women—patriarchy is alive and well. When our congressmen advocate for laws which restrict access to abortion, birth control, universal daycare and adequate paid maternity leave—and ours is the only country in the industrialized world that believes six weeks maternity leave is adequate for mother or child—they are practicing *male privilege*. When male religious leaders restrict women's role in the church, they are practicing *male privilege*.

So long as white men in positions of power make decisions which affect men and women of color—without proportionate representation from peoples of color—*white male privilege* is alive and well. When our congressmen advocate for laws which fail to ensure access to equal education and which limit employment opportunities and fair pay, resulting in unequal disadvantage to men and women of color, they are practicing *white male privilege*.

Perhaps the cruelest exercise of *male privilege* is when men decide to take us into war. Our front line troops are heavily laden with the poor and with people of color. It's rare to find the children of our ruling class fighting our wars, rarer still to find them wearing the boots on the ground.

Governments count the casualties among their military but the civilian casualties in war-torn nations are rarely counted and heavily female. Along with the dead, we must include "collateral damages": those who are raped or otherwise sexually brutalized; those who are wounded; those who have lost children to death or displacement and those who have lost homes, hope, and a future beyond despair.

But it isn't only *male privilege* that can be extrapolated from the *Wheel*. *Intimidation* is often used by our leaders as well. Before George W. Bush started the Iraq war he had to overcome public opposition. The public was told that Iraq had weapons of mass destruction; that the absence of war would end in a mushroom cloud. Fear of that result silenced many. But when protests persisted after the war began, the tactics of *intimidation* changed. The public then was told that if people didn't support the war, they didn't support our troops being sent to fight it. So, some citizens gave up their protests because they feared being seen as unpatriotic—of being unsupportive of troops who were ready to lay down their lives for them—even though a more effective way of supporting our troops might have been to insist they be brought home out of harm's way.

A more recent example of *intimidation* is the demonizing of the country's Affordable Healthcare Act. The public has been warned about everything from Death Panels to a FOX News commentator's insistence that pregnant women who are on Medicare will not be able to see their doctor of choice.

Although that last example is more a jaw dropping cause for amusement than fear this is how *intimidation* works. It is insidious in that it creates fear even though that isn't spelled out in black and white. For the battered woman *intimidation* threatens personal violence. For the public citizen in the above examples, it raises the specter of holocaust, of being thought less of by others, or of not getting the health care one needs.

A battered woman may flinch when her abuser waves around a gun, but the gun lobby *threatens* her security by promoting the idea that women need guns to protect themselves from men. A politician *coerces* a vote by explicitly predicting the dire results of voting for the opponent. Scarcity is used as a *threat* which subsequently turns us against each other; we're told that if our government helps out the "other", there won't be enough for us.

*Minimizing, denying and blaming* is everywhere evident in our social fabric. While pharmaceutical ads drone on with the mandatory warning of side effects, that possibility is *minimized* by the visual of happy smiling people who are enjoying their lives to the sound of soothing music in the background. When governments bring home the dead under cover of darkness they *deny* the effects of war. Political parties play an endless game: each *blaming* the other for anything they can think of instead of taking the responsibility for governing the country.

Dick Black, a Virginia legislator who was running for the United States Congress in early 2014, advocated for behavior from the rim of the *Wheel of Power and Control: Sexual and Physical Violence* when he argued that marital rape should not be a crime. He withdrew his candidacy after the American public expressed its outrage, but he is only one in a line of public officials and candidates for public office who have promoted *Sexual Violence* of women by suggesting (among other things) that they:

- Cannot be raped against their will.
- Cannot control their libidos.
- Cannot get pregnant if their rape was "legitimate".

*Isolation* is encouraged. Groups segmented and divided by gender, race, nationality, class, age and the differently abled, are demonized in some way to prevent their joining together to fight injustice. Just as her *isolation* makes it easier for the abuser to control his victim, *isolation* of the various factions in society is used to keep us divided and thus powerless.

Abusers use the tactics of the *Wheel* to control the behavior of their wives, girlfriends, partners and children but they see and feel the same tactics used to control their own lives even when they don't identify them as such. It should not be surprising then that their own behavior feels normal to them.

# Twelve

*"When we talk about equal pay for equal work, women in the workplace are beginning to catch up. If we keep going at this current rate, we will achieve full equality in about 475 years. I don't know about you but I can't wait that long.* -Lya Sorano

On no slice of the *Power and Control Wheel* pie is abuse of women quite so evidently transferable from an interpersonal situation to a societal one as it is on the slice labeled *Economic Abuse*. The infamous Equal Pay Day is celebrated every year. This is the day, most recently falling sometime in mid-April, on which women receive the equivalent pay that a man in similar circumstances received by December 31 of the preceding year. In other words, a woman must work three and a half months longer to receive the same amount of money as a man in a similar position.

All sorts of excuses are offered for this situation. Several of the more prevalent are:

 1.) A woman is less dependable because she may get pregnant.
 2.) A woman takes off work more often than a man to care for sick children or aging parents.
 3.) Women tend to work in lower paying "pink collar" positions, such as teachers or administrative assistants.

Nowhere is it clearer that women are still playing the men's game by the men's rules than in points one and two. Yes, women give birth. Since men can't, the only alternative seems to be to let the race die out. The pertinent, all-overriding question seems to be: whose children are these? Only men would conceptualize the practice of punishing women for performing an essential service to humanity that they themselves are *unable* to perform.

I will pursue the same line of thinking for point two except in this instance men are punishing women for performing an essential service to humanity that they themselves are *unwilling* to perform. There is no reason why men can't take time off to care for children or aging parents, and in some instances they do. But the pertinent observation is that these are essential services that someone must do, and, in a future world that ensures equality, commerce will accommodate those who perform essential services and adjust its pay scale accordingly.

Which brings me to point three and to the question: are these lines of work lower paying in and of themselves, or, are they valued less because they are traditionally considered to be women's work? An interesting fact to remember while sorting out that question is that men who work in what are thought of as traditionally women's fields, make more than the women in the same positions.

And what has made these fields "women's work" in the first place? Historically they were often the only fields open and available for women. Both historically and institutionally, men have prevented women from following professions that men have chosen for themselves. I will use the medical profession as an example because nowhere is this more evident than in the medical profession, especially in the United States.

If you go far enough back in history, medicine was the province of women. It was women who gathered the herbs; observed which had healing properties and for what; formulated the potions and handed that information down their female line so the knowledge was accumulative. It was women who assisted at the birth of babies and tended men's wounds when they came in from battle or hunting. It wasn't until men, in the form of Church and State, decided that medicine should be the province of males that women began to be pushed out of the vocation.[15]

Some women healers were known benignly as wise women or witches. It was not until after *The Malleus Maleficarum,* or *Hammer of Witches,* was written in 1484 by the Reverends Kramer and Sprenger, that witches were demonized and no longer considered wise women. All women healers became suspect of being witches, as described in *The Malleus* , and were subsequently killed by the thousands in Europe—usually by burning—with the sanction or direction of the church, both Catholic and Protestant. Of course, at issue then as now, was female sexuality. As conveyed by *The Malleus*:

*All witchcraft comes from carnal lust, which in women is insatiable. . .Wherefore for the sake of fulfilling their lusts they consort with devils. . .it is sufficiently clear that it is no matter for wonder that there are more women than men found infected with the heresy of witchcraft. . .And blessed be the Highest Who has so far preserved the male sex from so great a crime. . .*

So, if men could not control women's sexuality in any other way, they would turn the formerly benign witch and healer into a wicked being and any woman whose sexuality threatened them into a witch.

Traditionally, women healers were of the people and were the people's healers but the ruling classes wanted their own healers and in the Thirteenth Century medical education began to be offered in the universities of Europe. These were open to young men of means and strictly controlled by Catholic doctrine. From *Witches, Midwives and Nurses,* republished in 2010 by Barbara Ehrenreich and Deidre English:

*Medical students, like other scholarly young gentlemen, spent years studying Plato, Aristotle, and Christian theology. While a student, a doctor rarely saw any patients at all, and no experimentation of any kind was taught. . .Confronted with a sick person, the university-trained physician had little to go on but superstition. . .*

But nowhere else did the establishment go to such lengths to eliminate women from the healing arts as in the United States. On the rare occasion that a woman made it into a prestigious medical school, she was ostracized by the students and faculty alike. If she managed to graduate, she was barred from practicing in hospitals, and internships were not available to her. If she somehow made it into practice, her male colleagues refused to refer patients to her, or allow her into their professional societies.[16] Even though schools for lower-class women who sought to practice healing arts remained for a while, medicine was slowly becoming the exclusive province of men of means.

In 1910 midwifery was still widely practiced by women in the United States as it continues to be in other countries today. Pressure was put on state legislatures by the American Medical Association and, state by state, laws began to be passed to prohibit the practice of midwifery by any but professional—almost exclusively male—doctors; this, in spite of a 1912 report by a professor at John Hopkins indicating that most U. S. doctors were less competent than the midwives.[17]

The only avenue left for women in the practice of medicine was nursing, a far cry from the autonomous practice of the woman healer. She became the female nurse-helper to the male doctor-professional, and fell far down the pay scale of medical practitioners.

Today, the preponderance of physicians is still male. In a 2010 census of licensed physicians in the United States, twenty-nine percent were reported as women and the average pay for women physicians, even after adjusted for specialty, hours worked, and other factors, was reported as $17,000 less than for male physicians.[18]

Even so, the men must still be feeling threatened because a 2008 article in *Businessweek* asked the question: *Are There Too Many Women Doctors?*[19] The article asks if the shortage of physicians is due to women entering the profession and to the women preferring shorter working hours: average of forty-seven hours to the men's average sixty hours.

So, because women prefer not to work sixty hours a week, (usually because they are also performing essential services such as giving birth, child and/or elder care) they are blamed for a growing shortage of physicians. Women have become scapegoats for the increasing cost of a medical education, and the increasing red tape generated from the interference of big insurance, big pharma, and government, in the practice of medicine.

# Thirteen

*Whether they encounter violence in their homes, through their games, become abusers or victims themselves. Our children pay the greatest price for the violence in our world.*

My name is Dan. I am twenty six, single, and I was convicted recently because I tied up my girlfriend, Tammy. We'd been together for five months and one morning she just ups and tells me she's leaving me. Women don't leave me, I decide when the relationship is over.

I hit her in the head a couple of times and while she was still woozy I tied her to the bed and then I went to work. I had to do a shift and a half that day and when I got home, she looked really awful. She'd thrown up all over herself and messed in the bed because she couldn't get to the bathroom. She could barely speak and I untied her because I was afraid she was going to die. I helped her to the bathroom so she could clean herself up and then I went to get some food. When I got back she'd called the police. She isn't the only woman I've ever hit but she's the first to call the police

The people in this program I have to come to asked me if I'd seen any violence when I was growing up. Hell, yes, I saw violence. Some of my earliest memories are of dad slapping mom and of the two of them shouting at each other.

~

A woman may be able to tell me why she chooses to stay with her abuser. As an adult that is her choice to make. But the other victims in the situation, regrettably, seldom have any choice at all.

Children who grow up in abusive homes will carry those scars for the rest of their lives. Abusers argue: "The children never see. . ." but children always know. Children are completely dependent on their environment and the adults around them to provide for their needs. They are like small pieces of radar, honing in on any tension between adults because that is a threat to their own wellbeing.

They are also egocentric beings with a tendency to place the blame for the tension squarely where it doesn't belong—on themselves. Dan blamed his parents for ruining his life but he also blames himself for not being able to fix his family. Children will carry the shame and guilt of their family's violence into their own adulthood, even if they themselves have never been physically harmed.

~

When I was twelve, I got up one morning and found my mom lying half in and half out of the bathroom. Her entire face and everywhere on her body that I could see were covered with bruises and she couldn't get up. I ran to a neighbor's house and the neighbor called the police.

I rode to the hospital in the ambulance with my mom and then at the hospital I had to wait by myself in a waiting room for a long time. I have never been so scared. When they finally took me to see her, there was another woman with her and my mom told me that we weren't going home. That the woman was taking us to a battered women's shelter.

I hated the shelter. There were all these other women and all these crying kids and all these rules. I had to share a room with my mom and there was absolutely nowhere to go to be by myself. I kept begging my mom to take me home and after three days she did.

But the thing was, after we got home and all her bruises kept turning awful colors, I wished I hadn't asked to come home. I kind of blamed her for giving in. She should have had the guts to stay in the shelter in spite of me. My dad never beat her that badly again, but two years later they got a divorce and my dad asked for joint custody and got it.

~

When Dan's father asked for joint custody he was following a norm. Fathers who batter ask for joint or even sole custody, possibly because control of their children assists them to maintain some control over their former wives. They are likely to get it. Although all states have some legal prejudice against joint or sole custody by a perpetrator of domestic violence, most state codes are written allowing for rebuttal and/or judicial discretion and too many courts are still reluctant to come between a man and his children.

~

So then I had to spend half my time with my mom and half my time with him and try to keep everyone happy. By the time I was sixteen I hated them both so much for screwing up my life that I quit school and left home.

Since then I've just kind of bounced around. I've had lots of apartments and lots of roommates, sometimes women, sometimes men, and lots of jobs. I get bored easy and I've quit a lot of jobs but people just seem to like me—I can always find another one.

~

Although Dan denies being abused, according to a 2008 study by the New Hampshire Crimes Against Children Research

Center, children who grow up in violent homes are far more likely to experience abuse themselves. As well as being physically assaulted, they are also more likely to experience neglect, sexual abuse, and psychological abuse than children who did not grow up in violent homes.

There may be a variety of negative results from exposure to violence in the home whether the violence is experienced, observed, or only know to the child. Girls are more likely to have anxiety, depression, low self-esteem, and withdrawn behaviors. Boys are often aggressive, impulsive, and show anti-social behavior. Either may have poor peer relationships, poor academic performances, or show signs of post-traumatic stress disorder.

These effects do not necessarily end with childhood. An adult who grew up in a violent home is more likely to experience depression, low self-esteem and is more likely to use violence. An adult who was exposed to several risk factors in childhood such as child abuse, wife abuse in the home, substance abuse in the home or having a parent in jail, has an increased risk of developing major medical problems.

Sadder still is the generational cycle which assures that violence is perpetuated into the next generation as it has been in Dan's family. Eighty percent of men who abuse grew up in violent homes as did fifty percent of women who partner with abusers. No matter how much, as children, they may have hated the violence in their families, and even vowed that would never happen to them as adults, the behavior is, nonetheless, familiar to them and just feels natural.

Children who are exposed to abuse may, also, come to identify with the abusers. If they can get on the abuser's side, so to speak, it may give them a sense of safety and help lower their anxiety. What it may also do, as they begin to view the world as the abuser does, is give them an unhealthy image of the interactions of men and women and the roles they play in society.

With reluctance, Dan admits there might be some connection between his dad's violence and his own. But he states that women have got to expect it when they try to wear the pants in the family. This attitude may be reinforced outside the family, as well as in it.

Unfortunately, the violence children witness and experience in their homes is not the only violence in their lives. Most children are exposed to violence to an alarming degree even when their homes are peaceful. Our media bombards us with violence. After witnessing violence on television, small children behave more aggressively. By a child's adolescence, conscientious parents are hard pressed to limit the amount of violence available.

Marketing drives the exposure. Especially with television, the programming is designed to keep people watching between commercials and immobile during them, waiting for the action to continue. Violence desensitizes the human psyche so the advertisers must continue to increase it to keep our attention. And children are not only exposed to TV and movies but, also, violent video games.

A study by researchers at Simmons College, published in the spring/summer 2011 edition of *Journal of Children and Media*, found that children between the ages of seven and fifteen who play violent video games believe that some forms of violence are acceptable or even right. The study indicates that children's exposure to violent video games can impede the development of empathy and sympathy for others.

In 2008, the U.S. Army invested 50 million dollars in video games and gaming systems designed to train soldiers for war.[20] Overwhelmingly the soldiers being prepared for war, (in essence to kill), are men who will carry the effects of this training into civilian life and, indeed, for the rest of their lives.

If the Army thinks video games can prepare soldiers to kill the enemy, can we believe the violent games our children play are benign?

# Fourteen

*"And thus I clothe my naked villainy*
*With odd old ends stol'n out of holy writ*
*And seem a saint, when most I play the devil."*
**-William Shakespeare**

*My name is Stella. I am sixty two years old and I just attempted suicide for the third time in my life. I am also seeing my third counselor. I don't blame the counselors, they have all been good people. I just don't think what's broken in me is fixable.*

*The first time I tried to commit suicide I was only twenty three. I took a lot of pills that my doctor had prescribed for sleeping and depression; they made me very sick but I did not die. I did land in the psych ward of the hospital for a week and a half. They tried to be helpful but when I left the hospital they gave me more pills. I flushed the pills down the toilet as soon as I got home because I didn't want to ever be that sick again and I didn't really trust myself not to take them.*

*The second time I tried suicide I was forty eight. I had gotten married in the meantime, to a man who was abusive and who I finally divorced after seven years, but I had two kids with him, a girl and a boy.*

*My kids became my life for the next twenty years. They became my reason for living. If I thought of suicide in those years I quickly put it out of my mind. It wasn't until my kids left home and made lives for themselves that I tried to kill myself again. This time I did some research. I found a technique for taking just enough pills to knock me out, but not enough to make me sick, while at the same time using a plastic bag over my head so that I would suffocate in my sleep.*

*I just didn't realize how hard it would be to suffocate. I suppose I sealed the bag around my neck too soon because I must have clawed at the bag enough to let some air in before I was totally unconscious. I woke up ten hours later with the bag still taped around my neck. After that failure I went into a deep depression and eventually ended up in another psych ward.*

*I left that hospital, again with more pills, and I saw a counselor for two years after that. The counselor really tried; I really tried. I took my pills only as prescribed and I trudged through the next fourteen years of my life before I attempted to take it again.*

*It started when I was ten. I had two older brothers who were thirteen and fourteen and we had cousins who were older. My brothers took me to a park some distance from our house and when no one else was around they held me down on a picnic table inside a shelter house while my cousins took turns raping me. Our cousins paid my brothers for this and it was not a onetime occurrence.*

*My brothers said that if I told our mom and dad it would kill them. I told anyway. Not right away, but eventually I did tell Mom and Dad who didn't believe me. Dad beat me for telling lies about my brothers. I blamed myself for not telling them while I still had the bloody evidence that I had hidden and thrown away.*

*I think something in me was terribly wounded during the rapes. I think it died completely when my dad accused me of lying and hit me. What's maybe hardest of all; I think my mom had a suspicion the first time it happened, but she said nothing—not then, and not when Dad beat me.*

*I've talked to and listened to the counselors. I've gone to rape survivors' groups and talked to and listened to other women's stories. I've read books and watched videos. I know what I should be feeling.*

*But all I feel is worthless. The only time I've ever felt useful was when my kids were young and needed me. Now I've just become a depressed old woman who they have to deal with. Worthless to everyone. I can't even seem to be able to kill myself properly.*

~

The figures are staggering. An estimated one of every six female children and one of every ten male children under age twelve is raped, almost always by someone who is known to and trusted by them. When the rape is committed by a family member the numbers may be even higher because incest is believed to be the most underreported crime in our country, as well as worldwide.

The effects are staggering. A child has been harmed in the most intimate way possible with lifelong and life shattering consequences. In the case of incest a child has been betrayed by a family member—or in Stella's case—members: two big brothers whom she'd looked up to, her cousins, a dad who didn't believe her and punished her for telling the truth, a mom who probably knew and failed to protect or defend her.

~

*My name is Emily. My dad started coming into my bedroom when I was seven. At first he'd just touch me under my clothes but it wasn't long before he raped me. I used to imagine I was someplace else until he was finished. And, the next day when I went to school I couldn't believe that everyone didn't know. I felt so ashamed and dirty I thought it had to show.*

*When I got to be a little older and all my friends started talking about boys and sex I was always silent. I couldn't say anything for fear of revealing that I knew too much. Sometimes they noticed my silence and would tease me and say I just must not like boys. I didn't think I could ever possibly like boys in that way.*

*My dad stopped coming to my room after I got my period at twelve. After that he had nothing to do with me, inside or outside the bedroom. It was strange—I was relieved but in a way I felt rejected. I started trying to get boys to notice me, and they did. I let a boy have sex with me when I was fifteen, something I never thought I would do. When I was seventeen I got pregnant and I had my first abortion. The second abortion was only six months later but then I started being careful. I got pregnant again when I was nineteen and I kept the baby and married her dad.*

*The marriage was abusive—he beat me, just because. He didn't seem to need a reason although he always said it was my fault. I divorced him when my little girl was four. I didn't want her to go through what I had been through with my own dad. She's fifteen now and I've been super strict with her. I still don't like her being out of my sight. She just started dating and I won't let her go out with anyone until they've been to our home several times and I feel I know them well.*

*Since my divorce I've not had a man in my life. I think all men are pretty much the same when it comes to sex and I don't want to put my daughter in danger. I'm done with men. But I worry about my daughter constantly.*

~

The rape of a child by a parent or other household member is comparable to someone being held hostage and repeatedly tortured. How is the child to escape what's happening? Where could the child go to get away from this adult who holds all the power?

Stella's feelings of worthlessness and Emily's feelings of shame, are common reactions of children who do not understand what's happening to them and are helpless to prevent it. They think they must surely be worthless and shameful children for the people they love to be doing such unspeakable things to them.

These feelings carried into adulthood may lead to depression and the suicide attempts that Stella has made. And to the promiscuity and hyper-vigilance with her own daughter that we see in Emily's story. These feelings may also lead to self-mutilation or self-medication with drugs, or alcohol; eating disorders; and a lifelong struggle with self-esteem. These feelings may lead to one of several psychiatric diagnoses which are higher among victims of incest.

Incest is the hidden, hushed up, grimy underbelly of men's domination of women. Worldwide, little recognition is given to the immensity of this problem. As astounded as neighbors and friends may be to discover that the 'nice guy' living next door hits his wife, they do believe it. When they hear that the 'nice guy' has raped his nine-year-old daughter, however, their response is "No way, not this man, he would never do anything like that." And yet, statistically—and these are only the numbers we know—there are significant numbers of men doing something "like that."

Lot offered his virgin daughters to the Sodomites to be raped because his ownership of his daughters was total and unquestioned. The signs of ownership are still here but are more subtle. Many courts are reluctant to sever a man's paternal rights to his children even though he is a documented abuser of the children's mother.

There is still the understanding among many male groups: "my woman, my children, my house, my dog, my car," with no differentiation in the status of these categories. In some male groups this may be an unspoken assumption, but in others it is open and blatant. Some of these men, then, apparently need little justification for using "his", in the literal sense of ownership, daughter or son for sexual gratification.

As a society we don't know what to do with the information, the perpetrators, their victims, or their families. The information is often met with shock, re-traumatizing the victim. Perpetrators may be punished under the law, but only at the expense of testimony from the victim and, often, other family members. Indeed, many perpetrators charged are never brought to trial because their young victims are too traumatized to repeat the details of their assault to strangers. Families are given little support to work through the various feelings of guilt and shame.

When the incest is believed by friends and neighbors, excuses are often sought for the perpetrator. Wives are too cold, busy, distant, self-centered; children who are naturally cute, sweet and loving are suddenly labeled "provocative"; mothers are blamed for not knowing about the incest or for not knowing what to do about it. Once again, women are held responsible for the actions of men and victims are held responsible for their own victimization.

Incest is the ultimate symptom of male entitlement. Until the male-dominated society and its male-dominated family systems become obsolete, victims of incest will continue to face shock, disbelief, and blame rather than the immediate gentle support that will help them and their families heal. Only in an egalitarian society will we pass laws to punish the perpetrators of incest without re-traumatizing their victims.

# Fifteen

**"Damaged people are dangerous. They know they can survive."** –Josephine Hart

I have referred to women as "victims" throughout this book because I want to be very clear that in domestic violence and sexual assault there are victims of crime. In reality, I call the women with whom I've worked over the years survivors.

~

*My name is Chelsea. I married at sixteen. My husband's name was Bill and he was eighteen. He told me he was madly in love with me and worshipped the ground I walked on until I got pregnant.*

*He started calling a couple of times a day, checking up on me, and once or twice he came home in the middle of the day just to make sure I was there. He'd ask all kinds of questions about who I was with and where I'd gone and finally accused me of having had sex with another man; he said he didn't believe the baby was his. After that, he started hitting me. When he hit me in the stomach I ran away and went to the battered women's shelter. He called there looking for me but no one would tell him I was there.*

*The women in the shelter helped me a lot. They helped me get on food stamps and find a doctor for the pregnancy. The counselors there were helping me with interview skills so I could look for a job and all the women in the support group*

*helped me so much, just by telling me their stories and showing me I could make it on my own.*

*Then one day as I was leaving the shelter, Bill's sister was parked outside. She knew where the shelter was because she'd been in it herself once or twice. She told me that Bill was going to counseling and she said he was begging me to come home. So I left the shelter and went back.*

~

This can be one of the most frustrating aspects of working with domestic violence victims. Promising to go to counseling is an oft used ploy of batterers'. It happens so often that I used to wonder if there was a batterers' playbook somewhere with this information inside: Promise to go to counseling and she will come home.

In spite of my warnings to give it some time, to wait and see if he'll really stick with it, most women go back when he makes the promise. Most women do not want to leave their relationships, they only want the violence to stop.

~

*From my first day back, he never went to counseling again. Oh, he was real sorry at first but by the end of my second week home he had started hitting me again. I should have left the first time he did it because after I'd been home three weeks he beat me so badly I had to go to the emergency room. While I was there, I lost the baby, which I guess was what he wanted all along.*

*I called the women at the shelter and they came to the E.R. and took me back there. I stayed in the shelter ninety days which was their limit, but they helped me find transitional housing where I stayed another six months while I got my GED and found a job as a cashier in a supermarket.*

*Even after I left the shelter I kept going to the support and educational groups and I kept seeing a counselor there for a while, mostly because I felt so guilty about losing my baby. That wouldn't have happened if I hadn't gone back to Bill.*

*A year after I got out of the shelter, I enrolled in my first college class. I admired the women who worked at the shelter so much that I wanted to become a social worker so that I could help other women. I eventually got a graduate degree as well, but by that time I'd married a man who is a true partner. The sadness of my life has been that when Bill beat me that last time he did enough damage that I can no longer carry a child. But my husband and I adopted twin boys, who are now eight, and we have a good life.*

~

Many domestic violence victims struggle against great odds. Some of them remain victims but most can be called survivors because they have:

1) gotten out and started over, or,

2) weighed the choices and stayed, because for them, at that time, it was the best choice.

~

*My name is Ann. I had been married to my husband, Kevin, for ten years before he hit me. He'd always been controlling but he'd never hit me before. Then this one day he came home in a really bad mood: yelled at me, yelled at the kids, demanded the kids go to bed early so he could have some peace, and when I tried to ask him why he was so angry he slapped me hard enough to knock me backward and bruise my face. He said the turmoil in the house was just too much after a bad day at work and he blamed me for not controlling the kids.*

*The next morning we had near blizzard conditions outside but as soon as he left the house, I got the five kids together and drove us all to the battered women's shelter. We stayed there four weeks.*

*The women there helped me examine my options. I haven't worked since my second baby was born. He is a special needs child, as is my fourth, and I have chosen to stay home to care for them and to homeschool all my children even though I have a master's degree and I'm sure I could find work in my field.*

*I haven't had to work because Kevin provides well for us, but I know that if I left him he could not maintain a separate home for us and I would be forced to go to work and to put my children in daycare and school. I explored the various places available for special needs children and the daycare that might be available for my youngest, as well as comparing public school options with homeschooling for the other two children. I just didn't like the options.*

*The women in shelter talked to me about the effects on children of living in a violent home but, in all truth, I believed Kevin when he said it would never happen again and I had developed some skill at negotiating his tendency to be controlling.*

*I took my children and went back home. I did so believing that my being home with them and homeschooling were benefits which outweighed the sometimes tense atmosphere in our home. It has been six years since I returned and Kevin has not hit me again. He has no doubt that if he ever does, I will leave at once and it will be the for the last time. There will be no third chances.*

~

Both Chelsea and Ann are survivors. Chelsea because she got out and made a different life for herself, but Ann is a survivor too. She made the decision to return with her eyes wide open, willing to give her marriage another try because it gave her what she wanted, an opportunity to homeschool and care for her children herself.

~

*My name is Emily. You heard my story in chapter Fourteen but that wasn't the end of my story. I am now working with a counselor, an older woman who was herself a victim of incest. She is helping me loose the chains I have encircled around my daughter to keep her safe. She is helping me see that I must learn to trust my daughter to handle the responsibilities and freedoms that are normal for a fifteen year old so that she might grow to healthy adulthood.*

*With her help I am looking at the whole human race, male as well as female, on a continuum. Not all men are evil, not all women are victims. Once we are victims we need not stay victims our whole lives.*

*My primary focus will continue to be my daughter until she is grown and on her own. But my counselor is encouraging me to do some things just for myself. I have always wanted to learn to sew and I am saving to buy a sewing machine. I think I might like to try designing clothes, as well. We'll see.*

~

You may never know her story but be assured you know a survivor—or maybe several. They are strong women, with purpose, and a knowledge of the important stuff of life.

# Sixteen

*"When you rape, beat, maim, mutilate, burn, bury, and terrorize women, you destroy the essential life energy on the planet"* –Eve Ensler

1 Corinthians 13: *And then I shall see through a glass darkly, but later, face to face.*

Paul's message to the Corinthians was about love. And the passage may be interpreted as his inability to fully understand the love of God or God's son the Christ while in this earthly realm.

In 1961, the Swedish writer/director, Ingmar Bergman, used the phrase *Through a Glass Darkly* as the title of his Oscar Award winning movie. The movie followed four family members isolated together on an island for a twenty-four hour period, and illustrates how little we may know, even of our own family, without dramatic revelation.

I wish I could speak for all women. I know that the suppression of women, while not occurring in one fell swoop, was eventually universal and that oppression of women continues today across the globe. I know, as well, that my knowledge of violence in other cultures is limited; that I see through a glass darkly.

As I write, even as a woman I occupy a place of privilege. I am white, of Anglo-European descent and a natural-born citizen of the richest country on the earth. How then, could I presume to speak for women whose culture, mores, and treatment I cannot begin to know or to understand?

Even in my own country, the experiences of women of color, be they black, brown, yellow or red, will be different from my own and even when I know them personally I can only relate to their deep cultural influences through their stories. How much less, then, can I understand the dilemma of the Eastern Indian, African or Asian woman in her own society? How do I have the audacity to suggest that we should unite as sisters?

Let me return to Paul's message to the Corinthians, not as a religious exercise but as an historical one. We know the biblical message was cobbled together from six fragments of Paul's letters and that there are at least six more letters, so, without the full story we may make some assumptions from what we do know. At the time, Corinth was a large seaport, a center of commerce, known for its debauchery and violence. Paul was clearly concerned for its citizens. Against that background, Paul's message may be seen in a different light. Perhaps Paul suggests to the Corinthians that, rather than waiting to understand love clearly only after death, they should clear their vision and act in love in their present time because love in their present time was so grievously needed.[21]

Perhaps we need not clearly see each other's culture to unite against the violence which is the heritage of all women. Though I may never know all the forms of oppression in your culture, perhaps it is enough to know that you are oppressed. That the pain, fear and anger in the eyes of a beaten woman is the same from one side of the globe to the other.

What little personal experience I have had with violence against women in other cultures was during a three week service project in New Delhi, India in 1999, during which time I worked with women and children in one of New Delhi's shanty towns. I liked India. Its history and culture are rich, its people friendly, and the sounds, smells, tastes, and colors combine to create a sensual experience. I have always hoped to go back because there are many things to enjoy there—attitudes toward and treatment of women, however, are not among them.

During that brief period there were several newspaper reports of women dying in "kitchen fires": code for women being killed, often by their mothers-in-law or by their spouses at the mother-in-law's request. And of "Eve baiting", which is the practice of sexual harassment perpetrated by groups of young males against one or two females.

I also observed numerous signs advertising ultrasound services in many small shops along the streets. Ultrasound is extensively used non-medically to enable the abortion of female fetuses because girls are considered to be liabilities in that culture. Both India and China now face situations of having too many males for the females in their population because of extensive use of ultrasound and subsequent abortion of female fetuses. Until recently, China has had a one child per couple rule and if they can only have one child, a male child is much preferred.

Although my only firsthand knowledge may be of India—and that, admittedly limited—the World Health Organization (WHO) calls violence against women, in particular intimate partner violence and sexual violence, major public health problems and violations of women's human rights.

According to WHO's October, 2013 fact sheet, an average of thirty percent of all women who have been in a relationship report they have experienced some form of physical or sexual violence by their partner and, globally, as many as thirty-eight percent of murders of women are committed by an intimate partner.

Under "factors specifically associated with sexual violence perpetration", WHO lists:

- "beliefs in family honor and sexual purity;
- ideologies of male sexual entitlement;
- weak legal sanctions for sexual violence."

WHO further states, "The unequal position of women relative to men and the normative use of violence to resolve conflict are strongly associated with both intimate partner violence and non-partner sexual violence." And finally, legislation needed to achieve lasting change must: ". . .address discrimination against women; promote gender equality; support women; and help to move towards more peaceful cultural norms."

These statements are as applicable to our own country as they apparently are to the rest of the world. And remedies to the problems are, sadly, often lacking here as elsewhere. In 1979, The United Nations General Assembly adopted The Convention To Eliminate All Forms of Discrimination Against Women (CEDAW). This has been described as an international bill of rights for women and 187 of 194 countries have ratified it.

The United States is not one of the 187 but, instead, joins Sudan, South Sudan, Somalia, Iran, and two small Pacific Islands (Palau and Tonga) in its failure to ratify. Although CEDAW has twice been favorably voted on a bipartisan basis by the Senate Foreign Relations Committee, it has never been brought to the Senate for a vote.

There are other forms of violence against women worldwide which are not often experienced in the United States but may vary from place to place. These include femicide (the killing of women and female children because of their sex), forced and child marriage, female genital mutilation, maltreatment of widows and coerced sterilization.

Although I may work to correct the problems of inequity in my own society, when I see through a glass clearly, with love, I see that as long as women anywhere are in jeopardy

84

women everywhere are at risk. As we act locally we must not forget our sisters around the globe, even as we recognize their forms of violence may differ and their culture may require different solutions.

# Seventeen

*"Once in a while it really hits people that they don't have to experience the world in the way they have been told to."* -Alan Keightly

In an earlier chapter I said that the anthropologist, Claude Levy-Straus, attributes the subordination of women to the taking or bartering of women, tribe to tribe. This was both a violent act and a community action. The men, acting together, decided they had the right—*male entitlement*—to take or trade women, and they used violence to accomplish their ends.

Violence against women, then, is both a symptom and a tactic. It is a symptom of a system of domination which, although it may look different in different locales, is firmly in place worldwide. Violence is also a tactic which helps hold that system in place. The same may be said of all systems of domination be they racial, class, gender, sexual preference, age, or national origin.

In the BIP groups, we found it helpful to sensitize the men to the victimization in their own lives so that they might develop empathy for their victims. A discussion of power in our society usually led to a discussion of their workplaces which, in most cases, led to their discovery of their own feelings of oppression. Even men in middle management positions often felt squeezed by the demands of upper management, or "the corporation", the latter never used as a term of endearment. When they could relate the tactics of their bosses with how they treated their female partners, they saw power and control in a new light. Men could trace the wielding of power and its effects on its victims all the way down the hierarchical structure.

Did this mean they immediately embraced non-violence? Of course not. Lasting change of established behavior requires hard work, but they could, perhaps, begin to identify with their victims and recognize the societal forces which normalize power and control—not only in our homes, but throughout our society. And, perhaps, it could give them the incentive to do the hard work required to change behavior learned by the examples of societal violence, media influences, and—if they were especially unlucky—the example of their fathers.

The U.S. Institute for Peace's recent symposium on "Men, Peace, and Security," looked at how the ascribed norms of men and masculine identities contribute to violent conflict and concluded that the culture's indoctrination of men into hyper-masculinity may be the strongest contributing factor toward men's violence.

Christopher Kilmartin, a visiting psychology professor with the U.S. Air Force Academy, pointed out to the symposium that Americans tend to relate better to people who are victims of terrorist attacks or mass shootings than to victims of sexual abuse and that they are much more interested in funding programs to prevent the violence caused by terrorism than they are in funding programs to prevent the violence caused by rape. Over the past 12 years one trillion dollars has been spent on counterterrorism while the total sum of 2012's reauthorization of the Violence Against Women Act was 2.2 billion dollars.

Unfortunately, statistics show that women themselves are becoming more violent. This shouldn't be surprising. As women seek to become more successful and powerful on their own they still must navigate the violent world which men have wrought. Even though I was adamant in an earlier chapter that I didn't want to be a man, we still, as women, must negotiate in a man's world and play by men's rules. So we shouldn't be surprised when women attempt to be more *like* men in order to get along.

And once a woman makes the decision, consciously or unconsciously, to try to fit into the men's world, she must also accept the violence. A woman who is trying hard to be "one of the guys" will change her body and verbal language. She may become a football, wrestling, or boxing fan for the first time just to prove how much like a man she is. In short, she subscribes to the hyper-masculinity culture in order to get along and to get ahead. But women have the power to effect change without adopting hyper-masculinity for themselves.

Women in our society have won the right to vote; to own property, and to control and sell it themselves; to marry whom and if they choose; to control their sexuality and reproduction; and to work in any field for which they qualify— albeit for less money than men. Many of these rights have been achieved within the last one hundred years and they were accomplished by women working together.

It is probably not coincidental, then, that women are encouraged to categorize themselves into neat packages with impermeable boundaries keeping them from making common cause with each other. Perhaps the most obvious example is the boundary between the married and the single woman.

Having invented the institution of marriage to control women's sexual and reproductive functions and to ensure men's paternity rights, marriage was promoted as the norm for women. Women who remained single were seen as somehow deficient and given the derogatory title of "old maid". They were also more likely to be seen as deviant: unmarried women were far more likely to be burned as witches than were married women.

Today, many women choose not to marry, but marriage is still seen as the norm. Married women are, sometimes not so subtly, encouraged to be on guard against the single woman who, having no man of her own and surely wanting one, must be after hers. And certainly the married woman must guard her husband against the single woman who must be a temptation to him.

I witnessed an example of how a woman's marital status still maintains importance while attending a marching band contest. The names of the band directors were announced as each band took the field. Male directors were announced as "Bob Jones" with no prefix. Women directors, on the other hand, had "Mrs." attached to their names. Indeed, there is no male equivalent to indicate marital status. Men are never expected to change their personal identities in order to reflect the condition of being married.

So marriage may be the first division in female solidarity, but once married, procreation is expected. Women who choose to remain childless are often seen as not fulfilling a woman's destiny—another division. And women who dedicate their lives to careers while others devote theirs to caring for a man, home, and family, create a third division—isolating factors all.

The biggest isolator, however, may be class. Women who live in gated communities are, for the most part, completely isolated from women who work for minimum wage unless the latter provides labor for the former. They know little of each other's lives, pain, struggles, or joys, and are encouraged not to care.

The affluent woman cannot comprehend the deep weariness of the woman who labors in the affluent woman's home for six hours and then hurries off to a job at a supermarket, two bus transfers across town, where she stands on her feet for an additional eight hours before hurrying home to kiss her children goodnight—after which she checks their homework, does laundry, packs lunches, and prepares food that the children can warm up for the next day's dinner, before falling into bed to get five hours sleep.

The affluent woman may have deep grief; may be oppressed and controlled by her wealthy husband; may have been sexually or physically assaulted, or have lost children, but what the working woman sees is the comfort of her surroundings, the cost of her clothing which could feed the working woman's children for a month. Her cushy bed, the one she has not yet risen from when the working woman arrives at 6:00 a.m. to prepare breakfast for the affluent woman's husband and children.

And fear is encouraged on both sides. The affluent woman is told the economically disadvantaged woman is lazy and wants to live off the affluent woman's wealth (taxes). The impoverished woman sees the affluent woman's contempt and the political and economic power she has and fears it will be used against her (as it sometimes is).

Youth is prized and promoted; the young—or young appearing—woman more highly valued than the old. And women are divided still further by their sexual practices and preferences. All these factors, as well as the inclination of some women to affiliate with the male power structure, keep women from acting together to benefit all women.

# Eighteen

*"Every daring attempt to make a great change in existing conditions, every lofty vision of new possibilities for the human race, has been labeled utopian." -Emma Goldman*

I have no easy answers nor do I believe there are any. A three-millennia-old system will not be easily or quickly dismantled. But I do believe women have unrecognized allies. Many men can see the flaws in the patriarchal system and how it affects them. People of color, male and female, struggle with the white man's oppression as do white women. America no longer holds out a welcome sign to the immigrants that only several hundred years ago were her lifeblood. We have forgotten that we are not America's indigenous people; indeed, the white males in power have stripped America's indigenous people of their autonomy and relegated most of them to their own ghetto.

It would seem that we would all be natural allies: women, working class men, men and women of color, newly naturalized, indigenous, different sexual preferences, the differently-abled, the aging—all of the disenfranchised in our country. It would seem that we would all be happy to link arms in a common cause. It would seem that united we would be an unstoppable force.

And we would be.

One of the things that stops us is fear; fear of the unknown other is a self-preserving natural instinct. What is not natural is the way our fear is promoted and sustained from all the bastions of white male power and greed. Become aware of the messages from the halls of Congress and the halls of commerce alike. The twenty-four-hour news cycle reports, reiterates, and regurgitates seemingly endless threats of dire consequences from one source or another. We are constantly warned about each other.

 Gerda Lerner wrote "*The system of patriarchy can function only with the cooperation of women. This cooperation is secured by a variety of means: gender indoctrination; educational deprivation; the denial to women of knowledge of their history; the dividing of women, one from the other by defining 'respectability' and 'deviance' according to women's sexual activities; by restraints and outright coercion; by discrimination in access to economic resources and political power; and by awarding class privileges to conforming women.*"[22]

Now read Lerner's words again, substituting the minority of your choice, such as race, national origin, sexual preference, etc., for 'women,' and see if it doesn't also ring true. The patriarchy uses many of the same tactics to keep us *all* in our places. Just as divisions are encouraged between groups of women to keep us from uniting, so it is with all groups who might join in a mutually beneficial effort to dethrone the white male power structure.

In an earlier chapter I wrote about how intimidation and the threat of scarcity is used against us. But scarcity is not the real problem in our country. Greed is.

The role of capitalism is to maximize profit for shareholders by any legitimate means. The role of government is to moderate capitalism, not to climb into bed with it. The redistribution of wealth in a democracy is accomplished by a freely elected government which modulates the greed in corporate structures and among corporate executives by fair taxation. It also optimizes the opportunities of all its citizens to become economically healthy and contributing members of the community.

We cannot today claim to have a freely elected government. Our election campaigns have become circuses of excess, extending for longer and longer periods of time, with the prize going to whomever spends the most on promotion. Once elected, our officials can no longer call their consciences' their own, for they have sold them to the highest bidder in their efforts to be elected.

Taking the money out of politics is the place to begin. In his 2014 State of the Union Message, President Obama said, "*It should be the power of our vote, not the size of our bank accounts, that drives our democracy.*" The fact that Obama himself is the beneficiary of big money does not lesson the truth of his statement, although it may question his authority to make it.

Without big money support—heavily white and male—and with public money available to all who want to run for office, our elections will be flung wide open. Only then will we be able to elect officials who owe their allegiance to the people who vote for them.

Never underestimate the power of a vote. If all disenfranchised peoples were to vote as a block, this quiet revolution would effectively depose the white male power structure. That's all it would take. In several election cycles the faces of our leaders would begin to look more like the faces of our population.

The white male power structure and those who affiliate with it in order to gain power, know this is a threat; that's why legislation is promoted to keep oppressed groups from freely exercising their vote. Laws are passed to make voting as difficult as possible for minority groups. Voting districts are rezoned, difficult to obtain ID's are required, insufficient polling places and voting machines result in long lines which discourage those with insufficient time or stamina from voting.

I can hear the dissenting voices insisting that we can't change human nature, that humankind is predisposed to violence and greed. I won't argue the point but I do believe a ruling body which is widely representative of our population, given time, will change our culture for the better. As our culture changes, so will our relationships with each other and with the wider world.

As women begin, with an equal voice, making the laws that govern them, men will of necessity learn to respect and collaborate with women. As minorities of all kinds see themselves represented proportionately in the halls of power and laws which support them are advanced, they will see their opportunities broaden and their dreams come to fruition.

As we become more respectful and collaborative within our borders, our relationships outside those borders will change as well. Perhaps we can begin to lead by example rather than by might.

I began this book with domestic violence and I will end there. In a culture where the rules are made by women of all colors and persuasions alongside men of all colors and persuasions, in an attitude of cooperation rather than control, there will simply be no tolerance for interpersonal violence. In a culture exhibiting power with rather than power over; in a culture that raises its children to value respect rather than control, power and control in the home will no longer be an issue.

## Endnotes

[1]National Coalition Against Domestic Violence: public policy@ncadv.org

[2]Ibid

[3]Rape, Abuse, and Incest National Network

[4]Gerda Lerner, *The Creation of Patriarchy,* Oxford University Press, New York, N.Y.; 1986, pg. 47

[5]John Calvin, *Commentaries on the First Book of Moses called Genesis,* (trans. Rev. John King, Grand Rapids, Michigan, 1948) vol. 1, pg. 129

[6]Gerda Lerner, *The Creation of Patriarchy,* Oxford University Press, New York, N.Y.; 1986, pg. 213

[7]Nancy Lemon, *Domestic violence law: A comprehensive overview of cases and sources.* San Francisco, CA; Austin and Winfield; 1996

[8]Jackson Katz, *The Macho Paradox: Why Some Men Hurt Women and How All Men Can Help,* Sourcebooks, Naperville, IL; 2006

[9]Suzanne Brown, *Feminist History of Rape,* Washington Coalition of Sexual Assault Programs

[10]Gillian Greensite, *History of the Rape Crisis Movement,* CALCASA'S Publication of *Support for Survivors: Training for Sexual Assault Counselors*; 2003

[11]Ibid

[12]Ellen Pence, Shamita Das Dasgupta, *Re-Examining 'Battering': Are All Acts of Violence Against Intimate Partners the Same?,* Praxis International, Inc.; June 20, 2006

[13]Evansville, Indiana *Courier;* February 15, 1996

[14]Ellen Pence and Michael Paymar, *Education Groups for Men Who Batter-The Duluth Model,* Springer Publishing Co., New York, N.Y.; 1993

[15]Barbara Ehrenreich, Deidre English, *Witches, Midwives & Nurses,* 2nd edition; The Feminist Press, City University of New York, New York City, N.Y.; 2010, pg. 57

[16]Ibid, pg. 77

[17]Ibid, pg.86

[18]Rachel Emma Silverman, *The Juggle,* February, 3, 2011

[19]Catherine Arnst, *Are There Too Many Women Doctors?,* Bloomburg Businessweek Magazine, April 16, 2008

[20]Seth Robson, *Stars and Stripes,* November 23, 2008

[21]Rev. Dr. Claudia A. Ramisch, Unitarian Universalist Congregation of Owensboro, KY, personal consultation, November, 2013

[22]Gerda Lerner, *The Creation of Patriarchy,* Oxford University Press, New York, N.Y.; 1986, pg. 217

EPILOGUE

Even as I prepare this manuscript for publication the news is filled with stories of domestic violence and child abuse which are connected to the names of several prominent sports figures, notably, football players. As I write, the NFL has, reportedly, permanently suspended Ray Rice, a player for the Baltimore Ravens, for having committed a well-documented and well-publicized act of domestic violence. Adrian Peterson of the Minnesota Vikings has been suspended by the Vikings for an alleged act of child abuse, again documented with pictures and well-publicized, although it is reported that Peterson will still be paid. Taking the two incidents at face value, I would assume that the NFL considers domestic violence to be more serious than child abuse although I most sincerely hope I am mistaken in that assumption.

This, of course, is not the first time a prominent sports figure has been involved in either domestic violence or child abuse. If the average male feels a sense of entitlement regarding his female partner and his children, how much more entitled must the average sports hero feel while followed by millions of enthralled fans and being paid astronomical sums of money? These cannot be the only incidences of abuse. They are only the most recent that have come to light, and as much as domestic violence and child abuse are underreported in the average household, how much more so may they be in the multi-million dollar household?

The NFL's response has obviously been made to counter bad publicity and the pressure of its advertisers. What will be interesting to watch is its response when the newscasters have gone on to the next news cycle. They are in a position to effect real change, if they have the will to do so. Making a positive, on-going stand against domestic violence within hyper-masculinity's gold standard—football—and enlisting other sports' organizations to join them, could be a real start at changing a culture. Just as the knowledge that their football hero, O. J. Simpson, had been charged with domestic violence battery brought recognition of domestic violence to a generation, the NFL's ongoing active stand against it and child abuse could make committing violence against either women or children an abomination for another generation.

There will be no quick and easy fix. Once again, what has been three millennia in the making will not be resolved in a year or two. But the NFL has an opportunity. It will be interesting to see if the commitment of money, time and talent continues after the heat of publicity is off. That's when we'll know if the heart of the NFL has been changed or if it's back to business as usual. . .

## About the author

Marilyn Duncan first became interested in the battered women's movement in 1983 and spent twenty-one of the next thirty years working in this field. As a social worker, she has implemented services for victims of domestic violence and sexual assault; organized community responses to violence against women; planned and implemented rape prevention programs for schools; facilitated batterers' intervention programs; trained professionals, volunteers, and the public. As a writer, she has written training materials, speeches, short stories, an opinion column, and published her first novel, *While Good Men Sleep,* in 2013. She is currently working on a sequel to the novel.

Marilyn can be reached at:

mduncanauthor@gmail.com

or

www.marilynduncanbooks.com

www.ingramcontent.com/pod-product-compliance
Lightning Source LLC
Chambersburg PA
CBHW050405290526
45786CB00003B/1141